9/23/16

Mimi and Walter,
    With best wishes and
warmest regards.
                    Your Friend,
                    Bill Simon

"In *Great Catholic Parishes*, we hear the prophetic voices of pastors who have long labored with many coworkers to implement core parish practices that, if more broadly adopted, promise to revitalize Catholic parish life in the United States. The passionate and practical testimonies of these leaders are integrated into Bill Simon's insightful conclusions, resulting in the renewed vision of a magnificent mosaic that is taking shape in the Church today. Simon's zeal and hope for the future of parish life are contagious! This invaluable study should be shared with every ministry student preparing for ecclesial leadership today."

Jan Poorman
Director of Formation and Field Education in the Master of Divinity Program
University of Notre Dame

"An insightful look at what is going right in those parishes that are successfully nourishing their spiritual families."

From the foreword by **Cardinal Timothy M. Dolan**
Archbishop of New York

"This book may be the best catalyst ever for assisting Catholic parish life to be even better. It gives fascinating details on many of the best parishes in North America. It gives practical tips on how to improve hymns, homilies, architecure, liturgy—the works. It gives a tremendous boost to great pastors (especially the overworked and undersung). It covers virtually every aspect of parish life and is a powerful invitation to great lay people to pitch in. For most of us, the parish is the Church."

Michael Novak
Catholic philosopher, theologian, and author

"If you're looking for the components of vibrant parish life, and what you can do to make them happen in your parish, go no further. Bill Simon and his Parish Catalyst team have researched deeply and prescribed wisely. This is the book we parishioners (and our pastors) have been waiting for, so that we can make our parishes welcoming, vibrant, meaningful, and faith-filled."

Paul Wilkes
Author of *Excellent Catholic Parishes*

"The key to the New Evangelization is the renewal of the parish. Bill Simon is passionate about this, and my own parish has benefited directly from his passion. This book is a valuable contribution to the exciting and necessary conversation about parish vitality and revitalization that is sweeping through our Church."

Rev. James Mallon
Pastor of Saint Benedict Parish in Halifax, Nova Scotia
Author of *Divine Renovation*

"Bill Simon's practical wisdom and generous leadership are welcome gifts to the Church today. His latest book is an inspiring read and a useful resource for pastors and parish staffs looking to build healthy, growing parishes."

Rev. Michael White and Tom Corcoran
Authors of *Rebuilt*

A LIVING MOSAIC

GREAT CATHOLIC PARISHES

HOW FOUR ESSENTIAL PRACTICES MAKE THEM THRIVE

William E. Simon Jr.

Ave Maria Press AVE Notre Dame, Indiana

Founded in 1865, Ave Maria Press is a ministry of the United States Province of Holy Cross.

www.avemariapress.com

Paperback: ISBN-13 978-1-59471-417-7

E-book: ISBN-13 978-1-59471-418-4

Cover image © Thinkstock.com.

Cover and text design by Brian C. Conley.

Printed and bound in the United States of America.

Library of Congress Cataloging-in-Publication Data
Names: Simon, William E., 1951- author.
Title: Great Catholic parishes : a living mosaic : how four essential
  practices make them thrive / William E. Simon Jr.
Description: Notre Dame, IN : Ave Maria Press, 2016. | Includes
  bibliographical references.
Identifiers: LCCN 2016021630 (print) | LCCN 2016031715 (ebook) | ISBN
  9781594714177 (pbk.) | ISBN 9781594714184 (Ebook)
Subjects: LCSH: Church work--Catholic Church. | Church work--United States. |
  Catholic Church--United States. | Parishes--United States.
Classification: LCC BX2347 .S565 2016 (print) | LCC BX2347 (ebook) | DDC
  253/.3273--dc23
LC record available at https://lccn.loc.gov/2016021630

To the Body of Christ
as manifested in the
American Catholic parish.

CONTENTS

FOREWORD

There's nothing like a big celebration with family and friends. I'm sure you know what I mean; whether it's someone's birthday, anniversary, graduation, or some other special occasion, nothing beats the feeling of being surrounded by people you love and care for, sharing stories, maybe singing some favorite songs, and enjoying a great meal together.

Now, what if I said you were invited to a great celebration like this every week? Even better, what if I told you that the same group of people that join you at these great feasts were there to help you in difficult times as well: in times of need, suffering, and grief? In response, you might ask me where you can find these people and where all this activity takes place. And I'd tell you, "Stop by your local parish."

To be certain, this is not the experience that all Catholics have at their parishes today. However, this is an image of what parishes can and should be: the community and place where we celebrate that greatest of all feasts, the holy sacrifice of the Mass, and where we turn for comfort and grace through all of life's challenges. In this vision, the parish is truly our spiritual family, not just a group of near-strangers we briefly encounter once a week.

If you think this image of a parish is unrealistic, then this book is for you. Does the Catholic Church face many challenges today? Absolutely. But let's not forget that, in many places, the Church is vibrant and thriving. Soon you'll be reading about many of those parishes. *Great Catholic Parishes: A Living Mosaic* is an insightful look at what is going right in those parishes that are successfully nourishing their spiritual families. Even more, Bill Simon and his team approached this project in rigorous fashion—not just taking a few isolated stories but speaking with and analyzing data from nearly 250 parishes across the United States.

What they found, and what you'll soon learn, is that successful parishes have a number of common characteristics: they involve lay men and women in leadership roles; they pay special attention to Sunday Mass; they focus on developing the faith of their parishioners, thereby forming disciples; and they look outward into the community by finding ways to evangelize. Among this wide survey of pastors you will find a number of helpful approaches and insights that shed light on how to excel in these areas. You will also find a great deal of candor about ways in which even these parishes struggle and seek to do better. I think you will appreciate the balanced perspective that results, and I hope you will be challenged to keep improving your own parish.

I was blessed to grow up in a parish that exhibited many of these qualities that Bill Simon has identified in *Great Catholic Parishes*. Holy Infant in Ballwin, Missouri, was where I learned the faith from wonderful Sisters of Mercy, grew in my love for the Eucharist, and discerned that God called me to be a priest. I was fortunate to finish my studies for the priesthood in Rome, and when the time came for ordination, some of my classmates chose to be ordained in one of Rome's many magnificent churches. For me, however, the choice of where to be ordained was clear—at *my* parish. So I went back to Holy Infant, and my ordination day there remains among my most cherished memories. After all, what better place than my parish to celebrate a special occasion with family and friends?

Cardinal Timothy M. Dolan
Archbishop of New York

PREFACE

I'm waiting. My back pockets are parked firmly in a seat they've occupied weekly for twenty-five years. It's a place as comfortable and familiar as I figure we get in this life.

"If you would please join us in singing Psalm 27."

The music starts. It's not the traditional choral music I heard as a boy. It's digitized, multi-instrumental, and layered. The voice of the cantor sounds at once full and intimate.

"The Lord is my light and my salvation; whom should I fear?"

I crane my neck to look upward. It's Lent, and the limestone roof is illuminated in a distilled purple hue emanating from rows of LED bulbs and is cut with the amber shades of early evening's natural light pouring through the windows as the sun readies to retire below the Pacific Ocean after a long Sunday.

"The Lord is my life's refuge; of whom should I be afraid?"

Inside this Catholic church at Seventh and California Streets in Santa Monica, California, I'm joined by all kinds of people. It's now Communion time. Some of them process forward slowly. Many sing along. My gaze settles on the best sight of my week: the two-thousand-year-old line of the faithful. I watch the communicants return to their seats after receiving the Eucharist.

The first person I see is a short woman wearing a bright pink dress. Her features are firm but soft. The corners of her mouth are curled into a slight smile as she holds her hands in prayer and looks straight ahead. When she passes, a wave of floral perfume hits me just as the next person in line comes into view.

It's a mother, followed by her son. A pair of basketball shoes hangs over his shoulder. One sneaker narrowly misses the head of the person sitting in front of me. He does not, I should add, smell at all floral.

Next, a woman bolstering her sleeping toddler against her shoulder creaks open the side door near to me and slides outside. Her exit sends a ribbon of bronze sunlight across my pew.

People return from Communion at a speed that allows me to catch only brief details. From my seat up at the front on the left side of the church, I glimpse eyes cast down, eyes looking forward, a cradled baby, hands folded in prayer, a red polo shirt, flip-flops. People continue passing by, one by one, until it's finally my turn. I stand up. The guy in front of me has a waxed mustache, and the girl in front of him has tattoos on her forearms.

For a guy originally from New Jersey, where attending Mass used to mean suits and ties, it's a long way from home, but I feel comfortable with this crew. Most of them haven't had a "white light" experience. They get mad, fall short of their own expectations, and struggle with their vices. These people are my community—and I'm grateful to be in communion with them. The lady in pink, the basketball shoes, the tattoos and toddlers, myself and my family—we are a living mosaic. Our collage of experiences, aspirations, triumphs, and troubles forms the image of the Body of Christ in our time and place. It's my Catholic parish. It's an art form that the Holy Spirit has been assembling over and over again for nearly two thousand years.

Like most faith journeys, mine has had a few twists and turns along the way. I am a cradle Catholic. Both my mother and father were Catholic, and when I was a boy, I attended Mass every Sunday. All seven of us children got dressed up and piled in for the short drive to St. Teresa's Church in Summit, New Jersey—no questions or debate. It was what you did. I don't remember missing a Sunday Mass until I was probably about eighteen years old. I also attended the parish school up to eighth grade.

The first real twist in my road came during college. I went through an evangelical phase, followed by a Pentecostal one. After I graduated from Williams in 1973, I moved to New York City and began a real wilderness phase. Later, after law school, when I started working as an assistant United States attorney in New York, I found myself attending the 12:10 Mass at the parish next to work every day in an effort to ground myself. I was a seeker—there's no doubt—but a part of me was still just checking the box.

I moved with my family to Los Angeles for business in 1990, expecting to stay two years. As luck would have it, we were connected fairly quickly with St. Monica's Church in Santa Monica. A friend had recommended the parish, and I found myself drawn to Msgr. Lloyd Torgerson, the pastor who was, and still is, at St. Monica's helm. I'd never met a priest quite like him before. Several years later I found myself kneeling in the pews at St. Monica's, and for the first time I felt spiritually at home. I was thirty-nine and in need of solace. I was trying to find serenity and balance amid many obligations and a very busy life. With my brother, Peter, and my father, I was running a huge business, our oldest son had been diagnosed with autism, and things were coming at me from all sides. I'd go to St. Monica's, sometimes even without thinking about it. I confronted a few demons and found a lot of peace in those pews.

In 2002, at age fifty-one, I ran for governor of the state of California. My father had been secretary of the treasury under Presidents Nixon and Ford, so I'd had some early exposure to the world of politics and public service. I had always had it in the back of my mind that I might run for office one day, but I hadn't seriously considered it until the eve of the 2000 presidential election, when the chairman of the California Republican Party came to my office to request a donation for the George W. Bush presidential campaign. His casual suggestion that I run for office set things in motion.

For the next two years, I explored the possibility of running for governor, and then I entered the race. I won the Republican primary in March 2002 but lost the general election by a relatively close margin to the incumbent, Gray Davis. I found the entire experience intellectually and emotionally stimulating, but it left little time to develop my faith. I missed that greatly. I briefly entered the political fray again in 2007 as director of policy and speechwriting for Mayor Rudolph Giuliani's presidential campaign. Since then, I've focused on the investment business, William E. Simon & Sons, started with my father and brother in 1988, my philanthropic work, several foundations, and teaching at UCLA and USC.

Now my fascination with and passion for a number of other pursuits over the past forty years has largely shifted to a strong focus on my faith, my faith community, and faith communities all across the country. Through prayer and the help of a good spiritual director, I became aware that the Holy Spirit was putting people and opportunities in my path that have led this perennial religious seeker in ways I would never have imagined.

In 2012 I started Parish Catalyst, an organization devoted to supporting the health and development of Catholic parishes. This book contains some of the first fruits of that project; we want to share with all parishes what Parish Catalyst has found to be the self-reported best practices, opportunities, and challenges of more than two hundred excellent parishes. The outstanding pastors and staffs at these parishes have been a great inspiration to all of us at Parish Catalyst. It is for them and the people they shepherd that this book was written.

While my name appears alone on the cover, there are really a host of coauthors without whom this book would not exist. First and foremost, of course, are the 244 pastors across the country who devoted so much time to our interviews and who were wonderfully open and thoughtful with their responses to our survey questions. Claire Henning, Parish Catalyst's visionary executive director, was my muse and editor from beginning to end. Tamara Luque Black did an amazing job of research, distilling 244 interviews into the compelling findings we discuss in this book. David DeLambo was also helpful in the interview process, and Parish Catalyst staff members Joseph Dao, Therin Fenner, and Jordan Russell provided valuable assistance along the way.

Myriad people shared their insight and constructive criticism. As always, I owe much to my sounding-board-in-chief, my wife, Cindy.

Many others filled in a living mosaic of support and good counsel. At various times and in various ways, the following individuals helped make this book a reality: Wilkie Au, Frank Baxter, Randy Billups, Bob Buford, Denni Cohen, Brent Dolfo, Jane Dubzinski, Alex Dwyer, Veronica Galdamez, Cary Hemphill, Nathan Nambiar, Tim Nations, Mike Paz, Jim Piereson, Linda Stanley, Msgr. Lloyd Torgerson, Dave Travis, Rick Warren, and Tony Winston.

This book has been a labor of love from start to finish because of the quality and passion of the people with whom I have been privileged to work.

INTRODUCTION

WHY THE PARISH?
WHY THESE PARISHES?

Twenty years ago, I was at a point in my life when many of the goals and milestones that had guided my early adulthood began to feel less meaningful. I prayed for God to illuminate the path ahead and show me his plan for my future. I had a deep hunch that there was plenty of important work for me to do in the area of religion and faith, but I wondered: How could I best serve the Church?

The answer that came to me also assumed the form of a question: Where is Catholic faith experienced? Where has it been lived, day-to-day, by the most people for centuries? In the local community of believers. *In the parish.* As the United States Conference of Catholic Bishops writes, "Parishes are the home of the Christian community; they are the heart of our Church. Parishes are the place where God's people meet Jesus in word and sacrament and come in touch with the source of the Church's life."[1]

Millions of Americans are members of Catholic parishes right now—but they won't always be. Current trends suggest they'll depart in moderate but consistent numbers in the coming decades. They'll stay only if given reason to, only if there is something vibrant and life-giving in their parish, something that focuses their attention on the living Christ with such power that they cannot look away.

1

I know from personal experience how important a truly dynamic Catholic parish community can be to a person's life of faith. I was drawn to working with other Catholic pastors like my own, pastors who are skilled at leading and growing vibrant parishes. These religious innovators are beacons. They shed light on ways to address people who are still in the pews but may have an eye on the exit, and they continuously seek new ways to reach the growing numbers of unchurched people living within their parish boundaries. By supporting talented pastors in growing their gifts and leadership skills, we increase the chances that their parishes will continue to thrive and exert a healthy influence on other parish communities. I cannot imagine a worthier subject for exploration and investment than the American Catholic parish.

PARISH CATALYST

In 2011, I published my first book, *Living the Call: An Introduction to the Lay Vocation*, coauthored with theologian Michael Novak. The book focused on the increasingly significant role of the laity in parish life. Shortly after its publication, I received a phone call from an erudite and faith-filled Texan named Bob Buford. Bob's legacy in the evangelical tradition is well known. He was a successful cable television entrepreneur until he sold his business in 1996 to devote himself and his resources to what he refers to as "kingdom work." Previously, in 1984, he had founded and funded a small nonprofit called Leadership Network. By 2014—only three decades later—Leadership Network had grown to serve more than two hundred thousand church leaders all over the world. The organization's underlying strategy is essentially the same now as it was at the start—connect church innovators to one another to fuel further innovation. Bob had read my book and said to me, "I want you to consider taking Leadership Network's model to the Catholic tradition."

I soon learned that Leadership Network's first step was to seek out those pastors who have earned reputations as innovators—as pioneers or early adopters who create, test, and implement models of ministry that will shape the future of the Church. The next step was to bring them together with members of their leadership teams in small learning communities to pursue new ideas together—original thinking in parish ministry. Bob Buford will tell you that once you get the energetic and innovative leaders in a room together, all you have to do is pour coffee.[2] I would subsequently learn that there is a little more to it than that, but Bob's point is that these are the pastors who want to learn, who are already reading about, talking about, and testing different ministry models in their churches.

Because of my providential telephone conversation with Bob Buford and my introduction to the work of his Leadership Network, Parish Catalyst was born. In November 2012, Claire Henning, DMin, came on board as our executive director, bringing a great deal of experience in parish ministry. With my business background, Claire's parish expertise, and our many connections within the Catholic world, Parish Catalyst began to take shape.

In the first six months, we discovered that nothing like Leadership Network's process for incubating innovation existed in the Catholic world. Although there were (and are) many robust, effective organizations in the Catholic Church, we found no organization bringing strong, innovative parish leaders together for a deep and ongoing conversation about their ministry. This was a heart-stopping realization to come to after so many years competing in the business world, and it strengthened my resolve.

As we embarked, I was also guided by the wisdom of Dave Travis, who took over the helm of Leadership Network after Bob's retirement. Dave told me, "If you can impact 300 churches, you have changed the face of the American Catholic Church." There are more than seventeen thousand Catholic parishes in the United States— and we could potentially have a profound impact by working closely with 2 percent? This sounded eminently doable. So we rolled up our sleeves and got to work.

OUR RESEARCH METHODS

In 2013, Parish Catalyst reached out to diocesan offices, ministry leaders, and pastoral professionals across the country, asking them to name healthy, vibrant parishes and the pastors who lead them. This process generated an initial sample of more than a hundred exceptional pastors and parishes in the United States and one in Canada whom we then contacted and interviewed. The group grew from that point through "snowball sampling." This respondent recruitment technique, used widely in qualitative social research within the fields of anthropology and sociology, involves expanding a sample by asking respondents to suggest additional prospective participants.[3] In our case, this meant inviting our original group of interviewees to recommend other pastors and parishes they admired for their energy, spirit, and accomplishments.

The response to our requests for interviews was overwhelming: for every ten pastors we reached out to, more than eight agreed to participate in this first attempt to see whether Parish Catalyst's efforts might bear fruit. In the field of parish research, such a high rate of response is practically unheard of. This statistic is humbling because, while Parish Catalyst exists to serve and support pastors and parishes, our remarkable dataset would not exist without those pastors' generosity in sharing with us (and now with you) their time and their knowledge.

Our research team conducted a total of 244 interviews with pastors from every state in the United States. The geographic diversity of our parishes roughly mirrors the distribution of Catholic parishes across America.[4] We used an interview protocol developed with the help of Leadership Network and their thirty years of experience in interviewing church leaders. The goal was to create an environment—a context—for these interviews that would encourage the pastors to express themselves in their own words, on their own terms, based on their own unique experiences. We asked them to reflect on their major challenges and near-term goals and to share their greatest successes. We also asked about their leadership styles, their staffs, what gets them up in the morning, and where they look for inspiration. Once transcribed, the interviews offered more than 3,600 pages of information on life in exceptional American Catholic parishes.

We then analyzed this interview data, identifying patterns and common threads. Based on the pastors' thoughtful, candid responses to our open-ended questions, we were able to ascertain the most prevalent strengths and the most persistent challenges they experience in their parishes. This book represents our best effort to organize the wisdom gleaned from these interviews and to share our principal findings. In the chapters that follow, we present both descriptive statistics and quotations from the pastors that exemplify the trends we observed in this rich dataset. For more details about the research methodology behind our findings and our organization, please visit the Parish Catalyst website at ParishCatalyst.org.

OUR DATASET

Because we had such specific requirements for the pastors we wanted to interview, we did not expect them or their parishes to necessarily typify the Catholic Church in the United States. Nonetheless, the pastors ended up representing typical pastors in many respects, including their average age of roughly sixty years.[5] The pastors were largely diocesan priests, but many belonged to religious orders. Although we identified them as outstanding parish leaders who were shepherding some of the most successful parishes, they also expressed many of the typical concerns of any parish pastor: Mass attendance, finances, and staff interactions, to name a few.

Like the wider Church, the parishes in our study were diverse in terms of size, finances, and racial or ethnic composition. Approximately two-fifths (42 percent) were located in what they considered to be suburban neighborhoods, and roughly one-third (31 percent) were situated in urban centers. Twenty-two percent were in small towns, and 5 percent served rural communities. Just more than half of the parishes (51 percent) had schools associated with them. Their annual offertory collections ranged from $58,000 to $5,000,000, with a median of $1,000,000. For the full set of descriptive statistics about our pastors and parishes, please see appendix A.

OUR FINDINGS

Behind the 244 pastors we interviewed, there are 244 parish communities—each with its typical shares of challenges and concerns but
each also with its own wonderful story of vibrancy and engagement.
There is no single thread by which we can connect all these parishes;
there is no "silver bullet" for doing great parish ministry in the Catholic Church today. However, our research uncovered four essential
qualities that these communities have in common.

Our study revealed that great Catholic parishes (1) share leadership, (2) foster spiritual maturity and plan for discipleship, (3) excel on Sundays, and (4) evangelize in intentional, structured ways.
There is nothing revolutionary about these four practices. In fact, at
first glance they can appear deceptively simple. But these particular
parishes are thriving in a time and climate when many people no longer find value in organized religion. These pastors, parish leadership
teams, and parishioners have developed a clarity of vision. With a
deepened understanding of just how critical the Eucharistic celebration is to the mission of the Church, they have become strategic about
advancing the discipleship of their own people and the Gospel mandate to evangelize. The common attributes apparent in these pastors
and woven through these parish communities are collaborative, intentional, and joyful.

For all the good things happening in these thriving Catholic parishes, there is also unrealized potential. For every step forward, there
have been missteps. This book explores each of the four foundation-
al practices mentioned above in great detail. Each of the book's four
parts contains two chapters. The first chapters of each part (chapters
1, 3, 5, and 7) present strengths that the study's pastors reported on
the topics of leadership, spiritual maturity and discipleship, Sunday
worship, and evangelization. The second chapters (chapters 2, 4, 6,
and 8) name the challenges that these communities have experienced
along the way and continue to face. Each chapter highlights significant opportunities to make all American Catholic parishes more vibrant.

THE AMERICAN CATHOLIC PARISH

Like politics, religious practice is largely a local phenomenon. Though there are broad trends, Catholics generally practice their faith at their parishes. Undoubtedly, parishes face challenges in common, but to a great extent, each parish must develop strategies for that particular parish at a particular time in its history. A parish's approach to outreach, for example, is likely to be shaped by a variety of factors, including parish resources, the character of the surrounding neighborhood, and the demographics of the local population.

At the same time, each parish's strategies are embedded in and accountable to the universal Church and its mission. Keeping the bigger picture in mind and attempting to understand where we came from can help us navigate the issues that our parishes face today. For example, the Catholic Church in the United States has an interesting history: its immigrant beginnings in the late eighteenth century offer insight into the immigration concerns of the Church today. Before we turn to the innovations and insights the parishes of our study have to offer, we will take a brief look at the history of the American Catholic parish.

As Dr. James T. Fisher, a Fordham University professor of theology, wrote, at the beginning of the Revolutionary War in 1776, Catholics represented approximately 1 percent of the population of the thirteen colonies, an estimated total of 25,000 among 2.5 million.[6] The nation was largely Protestant, owing to the early colonies of the Huguenots (French Protestants) and Puritans (English settlers dissatisfied with the Church of England and having little goodwill toward Catholics). In 1789, several weeks after General George Washington was inaugurated as the first president of the United States, a Jesuit priest named Fr. John Carroll became the first American bishop of the Catholic Church.[7] With fewer than thirty priests in active service in the new nation at that time, a small body of his local peers elected Fr. Carroll to the office of bishop.[8]

At the parish level, Fr. Carroll inherited the trustee system, a democratic tradition that allowed elected laymen to govern the everyday matters of the Catholic community.[9] Given the scarcity of priests at this time, the system made a great deal of sense—but it presented a dilemma to the Vatican. It granted authority to affluent, influential members of the laity, leaving little voice to the poorer church members, those who often demonstrated much greater loyalty to Rome.[10]

In the early nineteenth century, the country was still predominantly Protestant. Catholics, influential or not, suffered from prejudice and suspicion. In fact, some of the most zealous defenders of the separation of church and state throughout our history were Protestants worried about Catholics gaining influence.[11] In 1820, while in Ireland, Bishop John England was appointed the first bishop of the new diocese of Charleston. Upon his arrival, Bishop England wrote that the Catholics in his diocese, which included North Carolina, South Carolina, and Georgia, were discriminated against and "morally degraded" by their Protestant compatriots.[12] In 1826, when he wrote the letter, Catholics were only 2 percent of the population of the United States.[13]

The scales were about to tip.

In the mid-1800s, the US Catholic population exploded due to waves of immigration from largely Catholic European countries. Although Irish, German, Polish, and Italian immigrants came in the largest numbers, there was also a significant influx of Slovak, Czech, Lithuanian, and Ukrainian Catholics.[14] As noted Notre Dame history professor Dr. Jay Dolan pointed out in his monumental two-volume work *The American Catholic Experience*, the greatest growth took place between 1820 and 1860, after which Catholicism became the largest single Christian denomination in the Northeast.[15] When the overall population of the Northeast doubled with immigration, the Catholic count quadrupled.[16] A region that had been only 2 percent Catholic when Bishop England wrote his letter was 20 percent Catholic a little more than thirty years later.

The process of immigrating to and integrating into a new country appears to have made these Catholics quite devout. As Dr. Fisher wrote, "Their hope for survival . . . was linked to their intense loyalty to the Catholic Church."[17] Though they worked hard to acclimate to American culture, the religious practice of these immigrant communities remained intensely bound to the Catholic cultures of the countries from which they came. Each immigrant group rallied around their nationality-based parish and lobbied to be led only by pastors who were members of the same immigrant group.[18]

The center for Catholicism became the city. Of the Irish population, 80 percent of whom had come from rural areas, only 6 percent settled in the American countryside.[19] Although Catholics' visibility within American society increased, their status did not. In some ways, the adversity Catholics encountered in the public realm shaped the development of parish life: the parish was their sanctuary. As Dr. Dolan puts it, the key to understanding American Catholicism is the parish.[20] The parish was the central gathering place for the people, the niche carved out of American culture for clusters of immigrants to celebrate not only their unpopular Catholicism but also their native tongues, saints, and devotions. According to Dolan, this was unique to the American setting. In other countries with Catholicism built into the national identity, the parish was not as central. In America, where Protestantism remained the "main vein of the nation's cultural bedrock," Catholics had to establish their own institutions in order for their traditions to live on.[21] Even in parishes of multiple nationalities, this phenomenon held; Catholics were united in that they experienced American culture through the lens of the Catholic parish.[22]

From 1880 to 1930, parishes multiplied across the northeastern United States.[23] The first wave was broken in 1925, when Congress restricted the numbers who could come in.[24] It was toward the end of this immigration explosion that Catholic schools proliferated, starting with the assertion of the Baltimore bishops in 1884 that "every Catholic child in the land" would have "the benefit of a Catholic school."[25] Prior to the establishment of these schools, Catholic children either received no education or attended public schools complete with Protestant prayers, hymns, and biblical translations. Among new immigrant groups, there also seemed to be a low level of religious knowledge that might be remedied by a Catholic education.[26] In the twenty years between 1880 and 1900, enrollment in Catholic elementary schools more than tripled from 405,000 students to more than 1.23 million. Religious women from more than forty religious communities staffed the schools.[27] Says Fisher, "The nationwide system of Catholic schools that resulted came to represent one of the greatest achievements in US religious history."[28]

As schools were added to a greater number of parishes, the power of the pastor increased because the school's budget and operating funds were under his control.[29] Further, as the school necessitated not only classrooms but also housing for the religious teaching staff, he became responsible for managing more facilities. As a result, considerable fundraising took place in parishes at this time. Beyond collecting free-will offerings, which were generally low due to the low status and low earnings of the average Catholic parishioner, pastors dreamt up lotteries, seat collections, pew rentals, bazaars, lecture series, and so on to raise needed funds.[30]

Perhaps relatedly, pastors began to serve long tenures—some upwards of fifty years—and accordingly knew their parishioners quite well.[31] Long tenures meant stability and familiarity within the parish. What was happening in the parishes and schools worked; the effectiveness of Catholic teaching and parish vitality likely influenced the significant increase in religious vocations experienced during the last two decades of the nineteenth century.[32]

In 1908, another corner was turned: in the apostolic constitution *Sapienti Consilio*, Pope Pius X effectively declared that the Church in the United States had outgrown its status as a "missionary territory." It was now considered of equal status to the Church in Italy, France, and Germany.[33]

A little more than a decade later, in 1921, immigration reform began, greatly slowing the Catholic Church's numerical increase in the United States.[34] This ushered in a season of stability and maturation, although there was internal migration as Catholics took part in frontier expansion. Catholic parishes in the West went from being missionary outposts (1850–1880) to managing a population explosion that caused a "vigorous era of building and fundraising once modern industrial culture took root out on the frontier (1880–1920)."[35] In the 1930s, expansion of facilities began to slow, and the average parish size increased to nearly three thousand parishioners.[36]

After the Second World War, Catholics were more likely than other Americans to move from the city to the suburb. Many also went to college. What had originally been a church for immigrants became a church of middle- and even upper-class people. Catholic parishes were no longer purely a product of the immigrant cultures that launched them—bastions of otherness—but a hybrid of those cultures and American culture.

Perhaps the greatest symbol of Catholics' full integration into American society arrived in 1960 with the election of President John F. Kennedy. More than four generations after Ireland's Great Famine and the 1848–1849 revolutions in the German Confederation spawned the first Catholic immigrant surge, the whole American Catholic enterprise was rooted, dynamic, and growing. Suddenly, it was "downright fashionable" to be Catholic[37]—and 25 percent of the population was. As Peter Steinfels wrote in *A People Adrift*, "[It would] have assuredly baffled those first generations of Americans . . . that by the middle of the twentieth century, Roman Catholicism, once alien creed, had become virtually identified with Americanism."[38]

Around this same time, from 1962 to 1965, the Second Vatican Council was held. Though it neither introduced new dogma nor uprooted any heresies, the Council was consequential. It renewed Catholic doctrine for a new, modern context; the Church would seek to engage the modern world, including other religions, rather than offer criticism. This was a true hinge for Catholic practice. The cultural shift reshaped not only Catholic Americans but also America itself. In 2015, six of nine members of the US Supreme Court were Catholic as well as a third of Congress and our vice president.[39]

Although Catholics have now become much more part of the mainstream, the history of the Catholic Church in America has been and continues to be the history of immigration. From small, almost negligible numbers at America's dawn, American Catholicism has swelled. As each new wave of foreign-born Catholics came to the United States, the domestic Church's root system grew, revitalized by new cultural devotions and deepened by those immigrants who left everything else but would not forsake their faith. The contemporary influx of Catholic immigrants from Latin America continues this trend.

For most of the last sixty years, the percentage of Catholics in the overall population has remained steady at nearly one-quarter of the total US population. However, a survey conducted by the Pew Research Center found that the percentage of adult Americans who continued to self-identify as Catholic had declined to 20.8 percent by 2014.[40] This decline raises the obvious question of whether it is a temporary dip or evidence of a long-term trend. Many experts speculate that this decline would be much larger were it not for the sizable influx of Catholic immigrants who compensate for American-born Catholics who have left the Church. In effect, new immigrants from Latin America, Africa, and Asia continually replenish the Catholic population in the United States. Indeed, one could argue that this influx of immigrants boosting Church numbers is part of a recurring historical pattern over the last 150 years.

Of the overall Catholic population, the number of those who are "parish-connected," as recorded in *The Official Catholic Directory,* is a bit smaller: 68.1 million individuals in 2015. This means that more than 80 percent of all self-identified Catholics affiliate in some way with a parish.[41] If you were a fisherman, the parish would be an ideal place to go fishing for Catholics; you can find most of them engaged in parish life in some way.

Where would the Catholics be if not in parishes? In today's social environment, being "culturally Catholic" is a common identification. Therefore, we can no longer assume that all self-identified Catholics are part of a parish or are practicing their faith. But many American Catholics, nearly 84 percent, are affiliating in some fashion with a parish, and across this country there are still many Catholics who continue to worship in their parishes.

Catholics reside in every region of the United States, though there remains a higher concentration of Catholics in the Northeast as well as in the southwestern and southern states that have a strong immigrant influence (e.g., California, Florida). Eighteen percent of Catholics in the United States are under age thirty; 41 percent are thirty to forty-nine years old; and 40 percent are age fifty or older. The racial and ethnic composition of the Catholic population is 65 percent non-Hispanic white, 30 percent Hispanic, 2 percent black, 2 percent Asian, and 2 percent other or mixed.[42]

During the abuse scandal that erupted in 2002, the negative public attention Catholicism received was considerable. As a result of financial settlements, parishes have seen a dramatic loss in support and services they used to rely on at the diocesan level. Eight dioceses in the United States have gone bankrupt. In 2007, in my own backyard, the Catholic Church in Los Angeles apologized for abuses by priests after 508 victims reached a record-breaking settlement worth $660 million, with an average of $1.3 million per plaintiff.[43] To afford the settlement, the archdiocese sold its headquarters, a twelve-story building that housed the diocesan offices, and then leased back only a few floors, curtailing many ministries. This, I am afraid, was not an isolated occurrence; across the country, services once available from the diocesan headquarters to help parishes and schools have shrunk dramatically.

Nonetheless, this is a storm the Church appears to be weathering. Here we are with a new pope providing an energetic and inspirational vision and still more than 80 million American Catholics,[44] the vast majority of whom remain on parish rolls.

GREAT CAUSE FOR HOPE

My first book sought to highlight the wonderful opportunities for laypeople to participate in the life of the Catholic Church amid negative public dialogue about the Church in this country. That book shared fruitful conversations I had with nine men and women who faithfully live out their lay vocations. Ultimately, this book is also about good news—about the places in the Catholic Church where creativity, vision, and devotion have the traction to move the mission of Jesus Christ forward. Despite the sensational headlines, there is great cause for hope in the Church, and I believe it is our calling as disciples of Jesus to point toward that hope whenever and wherever we see it.

If you are a pastor, parochial vicar, deacon, religious or lay ecclesial minister, staff member, or committed volunteer working in the Church, this book is intended to offer many practical ideas and more than a little encouragement. If you are a Catholic, anywhere from committed to indifferent, or from another faith tradition, I hope you find within these pages a renewed sense of commitment and energy for your own faith journey.

If you have distanced yourself from the Church or have never been affiliated at all, I'm thrilled to find you reading this. I welcome you to the conversation and hope that the faith stories and findings presented here help you better understand what Church-done-well has to offer the individual seeker, the community it gathers, and the world it goes out to serve.

As the writer Antoine de Saint-Exupéry said, "A pile of rocks ceases to be rock when somebody contemplates it with the idea of a cathedral in mind." More than a few cathedrals are sketched out on the pages that follow. Consider them well.

PART I

GREAT PARISHES SHARE LEADERSHIP

BEETHOVEN IN MY BACKYARD

After twenty-five years of Mass at St. Monica's, I can say with confidence that my pastor is amazingly welcoming to all people regardless of background. Msgr. Lloyd Torgerson has a tremendous ability to make people feel at home. He tends his sheep while also forging friendships and collegial ties beyond the Catholic community. I have run into people active in the local Jewish community who have said to me, "That monsignor over there, he's incredible. He goes all over; the guy is unstoppable."

People ask me, "What do you like so much about Mass at St. Monica's?" Now, there are a lot of different answers I could give. Instead, I usually ask them a hypothetical question. "If you knew Beethoven performed down the street, only a few hundred people attended, and every week he played a new piece he composed, do you think you'd go?" People smile and answer, "Of course I'd go." That's how I feel about Msgr. Torgerson; he is Beethoven in my backyard.

Overall, Msgr. Torgerson is a strong leader. Why is this? It's hard to capture leadership in a series of specifics, and as we will discuss below, there are many different leadership styles. One commonality is that good leaders are skilled communicators—individuals who are not only verbally eloquent but also able to communicate to others on a deeper level. They articulate a compelling vision and arouse strong emotional support in those they lead.

After attending St. Monica's with me for several years, my wife converted to the Catholic faith. At the time she told me, "Honey, I want you to know one thing: it had nothing to do with you."

It surely was God and Msgr. Torgerson—Beethoven in my own backyard.

1
—

THE NOT-SO-LONE RANGER

We have unanimity in heart and an ambition in mind of what we should be, how we should be as a parish.

—Fr. John Hynes
St. Catherine of Siena, Wilmington, Delaware

Our people buy into the fact that parish priests can't do everything, and so they step up to the plate.

—Fr. Dan Swift
St. Benedict, Holmdel, New Jersey

President John Quincy Adams once said, "If your actions inspire others to dream more, learn more, do more, and become more, you are a leader." Although we did not ask pastors to talk to us about Pope Francis, he was brought up spontaneously in roughly one out of every three interviews.[1]

Without exception, remarks about the pope were positive, optimistic, and laudatory. It shows just how effective a leader the pope has become for these pastors. My pastor, Msgr. Torgerson, remarked, "We've got a pope right now that, if a PR firm spent a billion dollars, they couldn't create what we've got." Pope Francis models faith and creates a clear direction for the Church that local leaders can communicate and local communities can embrace.

LEADING AS FRANCIS DOES

The pope's unique leadership style influences pastors at these vibrant parishes on a daily basis. Fr. Louis Vallone, who pastors both St. John of God and St. Catherine of Siena parishes in McKees Rocks, Pennsylvania, described the pope's overall impact:

> I've been waiting for this guy all my life. And in ten months, he's changed my spiritual life. The first thing I do every morning when I get up is go to the Vatican webpage, and my pastor preaches to me first before I go to Mass to preach to my people. I read his homilies every day. I read everything that he says and is reported. He is pastoring me and pastoring our whole Church. I entered the Church before the Second Vatican Council, became a seminarian under John XXIII, and I've spent forty years saying, "This wasn't the cruise that I signed up for." And now, praise God, I've lived long enough to see a validation of what was in my heart that long ago.

The enthusiastic wave surrounding the pope is, in part, a testament to his exceptional leadership skills.

Indeed, since his papacy began, Pope Francis has led through example and encouraged others to do the same. As Fr. Brian O'Toole of Our Lady of the Holy Rosary and Sacred Heart parishes in Gardner, Massachusetts, explained, "Pope Francis has become such a rock star because he's talking the language of leadership. He's talking the mission of who we are, of who we're supposed to be in the world—not just theologically but practically. He's telling the bishops this. He's telling the cardinals this. And if you didn't get the message, look how he's living himself. He's modeling the mission."

The Holy Father's comment that one must be with the sheep and smell like the sheep caught the imaginations of several pastors in our study. He inspires pastors to get out of the rectory and lead from the middle, with the help of others, including lay staff and volunteers. As

Fr. Jeff McGowan of Queen of Peace parish in Gainesville, Florida, echoed, "If you're not with the people so much that you smell like them, you're spending too much time in your office." The importance of pastors interacting more with parishioners and their communities is something we will examine at greater length in part III, where we examine a pastor's presence more closely.

Pope Francis's leadership style is highly collaborative. He commissioned a working group of eight cardinals from outside the Roman Curia to advise him on adopting changes in the structure of the Curia and the global Church. Another example of his collaborative leadership style is his interest in hearing voices of the laity as well as of non-Catholics at the synod he called on family life.

COLLABORATORS, DELEGATORS, CONSULTERS

Most of the pastors we interviewed (80.3 percent) said that the leadership models used in their parishes is one of their greatest strengths. Eighty percent of our pastors also said they had some form of shared leadership structure in place. Although, canonically, pastors are held responsible for all decisions made in a parish,[2] these pastors were quick to admit that they do not lead their vibrant parishes on their own.

In our dataset, shared leadership always involved laypeople in some way. The benefits are twofold. For one, shared leadership empowers laypeople to participate in parish governance, contributing valuable skills and unique perspectives to the parish. Second, shared leadership takes pressure off of the pastor, allowing him time to devote to essential pastoral duties as well as self-care. Lone rangers are no longer the norm in vibrant parishes.

As leadership expert Jim Collins writes in his book *Good to Great*, "The old adage 'People are your most important asset' turns out to be wrong. People are not your most important asset. The *right* people are."[3] Our pastors have a gift for identifying and inviting capable people to share the reins of leadership, and they place these people in positions that make the best use of their strengths. "We're blessed with very talented and generous people," said Fr. Kevin Duggan of

Mary, Queen of Peace in Sammamish, Washington. "We've made a real, concerted effort to try to attract and keep talented staff members by building a respectful and collaborative atmosphere for the staff."

We identified three different styles of leadership sharing: the collaborators, the delegators, and the consulters.[4] Many of the pastors in our study combined these styles, but most reported a dominant tendency toward one of the three (see figure 1.1).

- *52 percent of our pastors said they are collaborators.* Collaborative leaders value teamwork, cooperation, and consensus. The pastor and his staff work together as a cohesive unit.

- *49 percent said they are delegators.* Delegators empower others to lead by delegating responsibilities and offering support, encouragement, and freedom. Pastors who practice this style hire talented people, discern their gifts, and then allow them to lead in their areas of responsibility without micromanaging their work.

- *24 percent said they are consulters.* Consultative leaders emphasize the importance of seeking out perspectives and opinions that can inform their own decision making. These pastors see input, discussion, and deliberation as crucial to clarifying their vision and securing buy-in from the leadership team and the broader parish community.

True shared leadership in ministry does not happen simply because people work together or cooperate with one another in some way. It is a gradual and mutual evolution of new patterns. The shift to shared leadership represents a marked change from the traditional lone-ranger model of pastoring.

Figure 1.1 Three most common leadership styles

COLLABORATOR   DELEGATOR   CONSULTER

COLLABORATIVE LEADERS

Collaborative leaders value teamwork, cooperation, and consensus. The pastor and his staff work together as a cohesive unit. "I'm in the mix of it all, from administration to ministry to schools," said Msgr. Torgerson of St. Monica's in Santa Monica, California. "I rely hugely on our lay staff for all the parts, for both schools as well as for the parish. Structurally, we have a pretty collaborative style. We meet regularly once a week with senior staff. We meet every two weeks with the full staff. We have a parish council and a financial council and a whole variety of other ministry councils. I have a parish administrator who does a lot of the actual administration, but I'm still right in the middle of it."

Consensus comes to the forefront with other pastors who consider themselves collaborators. Fr. Bill Stenzel of St. Mary of Celle parish in Berwyn, Illinois, labeled himself a collaborative consensus builder:

> My preferred way of describing pastoring in general is that at any given time with people we're always founding a local church. My discovery a long time ago was that people tend to think of the people from one hundred years ago that founded the parish, but when you look at the history there are demographic shifts and turnover of populations. The first people that were in the parish under that name were the ones who signed the mortgage for several generations of parishioners. The essence is that people at any given time find themselves at one place, and the task is to discover what it means for those of us who are here now? We know the stories of what people who *were* here did. What [does] it mean for us who are here now?

The very question "What does it mean for us who are here now?" is a question that a lone-ranger-style leader cannot answer. To discover new meaning, a leader must be open to many voices and willing to collaborate. Effectively leading a parish today requires communication,

cooperation, consensus building, and teamwork. In our study, half
of these effective leaders found collaboration to be the best form of
leadership for accomplishing their mission.

DELEGATING LEADERS

If building a consensus is pivotal for collaborative leaders, offering
support, encouragement, and freedom is essential for pastors who
described themselves as delegators. They empower others by delegating responsibility. Delegator pastors hire talented people, discern
their gifts, and then get out of their way.

These pastors avoid getting themselves too involved in certain areas when they can serve better elsewhere. "I don't run the parish; I
lead the parish. My staff and volunteers run the parish," said Fr. An-
drew Kemberling of St. Thomas More parish in Centennial, Colorado.
"I'm trained to be a principal. That's how principals run a high school.
I don't teach chemistry." Similarly, other delegator pastors we spoke
to consider their tendency to rely on others a personal strength that
makes for a healthy parish.

These pastors avoid micromanaging and enable their staffs by listening to and supporting their decisions. Delegators appreciate that
some of the people they work with will have their own way of doing
things. They support staff members as they work through difficult situations, stepping in only when necessary.

Msgr. Pablo Navarro from St. John Neumann parish in Miami,
Florida, described his delegative leadership this way: "I try to lead
primarily through others. I try to pastor pastors. If it were not for the
very involved laity that we have taking responsibility in their ministries, there would be no way that we could do what we do. I basically
do the bulk of leadership and pastoring, by example but definitely by
collegiality and delegation, through the parish council, finance council, and coordinators of ministries. It sounds so bookish, but that's
what it is." Councils and colleagues exist for a reason. Delegative
leaders remember that and rely on others accordingly.

The councils described by Msgr. Navarro exemplify resources
that a delegator pastor understands and empowers for the good of the

parish. The delegator pastor manages time and his personal ministry more effectively by making way for competent staff and volunteers.

CONSULTATIVE LEADERS

Nearly a quarter of pastors considered themselves consultative leaders. Whereas the delegators lead through others, consultative leaders gather many perspectives and opinions to inform their own decision making. Essentially, their leadership is a living mosaic of those who counsel them. These pastors see input, discussion, and deliberation as crucial to clarifying the parish's vision and securing buy-in from the leadership team as well as the broader parish community.

These pastors consider themselves decisive leaders who confer with others at serious length and depth to be more discerning. "I get as much information as I can, as quickly as I can. I mull it over, listen to lots of people, and decide," said Fr. Charles Bober, pastor of St. Killian parish in Cranberry Township, Pennsylvania. He recognizes that decision making must be a daily occurrence because tomorrow will bring a new set of problems and decisions. Consultative pastors are confident about making decisions themselves but rely heavily on drawing laity into the decision-making process.

Fr. Volney DeRosia of St. Patrick's parish in Pelham, New Hampshire, described his consultative leadership this way: "I typically try to get as much information as I can about what's going on from different people, asking for a lot of different perspectives. And very often, I won't make a decision that could possibly be questionable without getting the input of the staff and pastoral council or school board and principal." This approach not only allows the pastor to make the best decision for the parish but it helps maintain a good rapport with parishioners.

A full 80 percent of pastors interviewed used one or more of the three shared leadership styles indicated above. Many used different versions of shared leadership depending on the situation at hand. Whether collaborative, delegative, or consultative, pastors said that their own leadership style was most effective when parish leadership positions were staffed with strong professional people. When pastors have strong professional staffs, they can rely on them to make major decisions and get things done.

Used effectively, all three shared leadership styles enable the whole community to demonstrate a sense of ownership and stewardship for the parish, allowing the community to grow organically. More members of the community become committed and engaged. Talented staff and parishioners are provided a path to leadership of their parish. It is akin to the experience employees have when they are offered stock options in a business: belonging brings more tangible rewards. Shared leadership gives the talented people already in the pews a means to participate more fully.

LISTENING TO LAY VOICES

Lay leadership is fundamental to the success of vibrant parishes. It came up as a topic in the vast majority of interviews because these parishes are sustained in part by competent, dedicated, and generous laypeople. Sixty-seven percent of the pastors specifically named their lay leaders as a major asset of their parishes and emphasized how integral they are to advancing their parishes' missions.

I first examined lay leadership in my book *Living the Call*. In my lifetime, the responsibilities resting on lay shoulders in the Church have increased considerably, and they will likely continue to increase as the number of Catholics in the country rises while the number of priests and pastors decreases. The old model of parish leadership—the model pervasive during my father and mother's generation and even part of my young adulthood—was "pray, pay, and obey." The layperson's script had been written and handed down. There was little more one could offer than its recitation.

The Second Vatican Council (October 1962–December 1965) prepared the way for change. One of the first issues considered by the council concerned laypeople and the greater role they could play in parish life. Ultimately, many of the roles that had been exclusively performed by priests before the council became the pastoral work of the laity: parish administration, sacramental preparation, liturgical planning, spiritual direction, faith formation, catechesis, and even

limited preaching. In most parishes today, it is a layperson who is the
first point of contact for anyone who comes to a church with a pastoral
need. The importance of this is hard to understate in describing the
changing reality of the American Catholic parish. In 2005—fifty years
after the Second Vatican Council—the Center for Applied Research
in the Apostolate (CARA) reported that 39,651 lay ecclesial ministers
were working in Catholic parishes.[5]

Lay leadership matters in the American Catholic parish. Teamwork and communication have become essential to decision-making
processes. Listening to advice from lay leaders means opening up a
lane for dialogue—making communication a two-way street. "I have
very talented people in the parish and they run the meetings," explained Fr. Michael Woods of All Saints parish in Knoxville, Tennessee. "That's their gift. I'm available; I'm there to listen and to guide."

Pastors work toward making collaboration with their staffs intentional. They are mindful of advice and counsel given by leadership
committees, which helps them maintain a balanced vision of the parish's hopes and dreams alongside their own. Following through, they
look for wisdom within the group and discuss an issue until a solution
is found. Fr. Dennis Carver, who rectors Nativity of the Blessed Virgin Mary Cathedral in Biloxi, Mississippi, put it plainly: "The pastoral
council is very strong. I take their advice and learn from them. They're
advisory and very helpful in attending to the needs of the parish. They
give me advice on what the parish's needs are."

Sometimes the advice is more prescriptive, coming in an area in
which a pastor might recognize he is lacking. No pastor is good at
everything. Pastors who are strong on providing pastoral care but
are weak administrators can rise or fall with their leadership team.
If a weak administrator can delegate to someone else who is better,
the parish can remain healthy. If a weak administrator cannot find
anyone to take on that responsibility, problems will pile up quickly.
In healthy parishes, the strengths of the team members complement
each other. Just having good people around is not enough. It is necessary to have people with the right skills in the right roles.

Fr. Carl Schlichte, O.P., pastor of St. Catherine of Siena Newman Center in Salt Lake City, Utah, described himself as administratively weak but good at interacting with parishioners. After some major reorganizing at his parish, he learned that parishioners forgave his administrative shortcomings because they trusted him. "A number of parishioners came forward and said, 'Let us help you.' So I have a kitchen cabinet that's made up of a retired accountant, a semiretired human resources professional, and a semiretired organizational management professional," he said. "[I say] to these folks, 'Okay, this is what I want. This is how I would like it to run.' And they're like, 'Okay, you need to do this, this, and this.' By myself, I'd be beating my head against the wall for a year to come up with half this stuff that they know professionally." Like all of us who employ a mechanic to fix our cars or a doctor to diagnose our illnesses, this pastor relies on the wisdom of professionals in carrying out the work of his parish.

Working through their strengths, lay leaders help a parish redefine itself. Fr. Daniel White, S.J., at St. Francis Xavier College Church in St. Louis, Missouri, said, "Allowing the lay folks in the congregation to challenge people where they need to be challenged and encourage them when they need encouragement allows them to have ownership of the place. Nourishing that sense of ownership is something we've always seen as a great strength."

Just as exercising strengthens a muscle, when parishioners and staff use their natural leadership abilities and personal faith to further the mission of the parish, they become more engaged in both leadership and their own faith development. Being open to outside advice, using a shared leadership style, and introducing lay leadership opportunities, our pastors have paved the way for individuals to engage their faith and leadership potential simultaneously.

THE DOMINO EFFECT

Lay involvement has had a domino effect in some parishes. Pastors have watched staff members empower volunteers to become leaders themselves, eventually taking on special projects and programs in the parish. Over time, parishes form a tradition of lay involvement.

Pastors mentioned that parishioners become accustomed to getting involved and exercising leadership. "Here, people will notice something and say 'You know, we really should do that, and I'd be willing to take that on,'" noted Fr. John Bergstadt about the contagious lay involvement at St. John the Baptist parish in Green Bay, Wisconsin. "That, to me, is a huge difference."

Another domino effect is the proliferation of parish ministries with the advent of increased lay involvement. There no longer needs to be a one-size-fits-all template to maximize a pastor's economy of scale. Some parishes we interviewed reported as many as one hundred ministries active in their parish—something unheard of only two generations ago.

PRAISE FOR LAY LEADERS

Over and over we heard from pastors who heaped praise on laypeople who excelled in leadership roles. Staff members and ministry leaders were lauded by name and title for their excellent contributions to the work of the parish. "We have a wonderful stewardship director," said Fr. Tom Lilly of St. Elizabeth Ann Seton parish in Anchorage, Alaska. "He constantly encourages ministries throughout the parish, highlighting what they do and inviting new members into that." Others praised their music directors and pastoral associates. Certain staff members are a godsend to pastors in need of help in a specific area. "I know that I know little about finances," Fr. T. Mathew Rowgh from St. Agnes parish in Shepherdstown, West Virginia, explained. "I have a wonderful finance council. They know that I have no interest in this. I don't sit and look at the figures. I don't even know what I'm looking at when I look at the figures. They know what they're doing; they've been in business and so on." Other staff members simply help straighten out the complicated duties of a pastor, as Fr. George Witt, S.J., of St. Ignatius Loyola in New York City has found: "I have a wonderful assistant who is a total type A, detail-orientated person. Her presence is so important to this parish." These lay leaders, brought up voluntarily by the pastors, were praised for the major contributions they made to the health and vitality of the parishes they serve.

These testimonies show that one layperson in the right position can have a remarkable influence on the parish as a whole. Fr. William Kenny of Holy Spirit parish in Las Vegas, Nevada, described how his parish's excellent youth minister identified so well with high-school students that they brought their families with them to church. A staff member at Assumption parish in O'Fallon, Missouri, launched an informal leadership program on her own. Fr. Joseph Kempf explained in detail:

> [The staff member] is our religion coordinator for our school and has a counseling background and experience. She also is in charge of leadership development. With other staff members she has leadership training days [and] occasional training bulletins, and she'll email the leaders. We have recently begun to invite each organization to develop a mission statement for themselves. She created a lovely little PowerPoint which walks you through it. She and our other pastoral staff persons have sat down face-to-face with each person involved in coordinating a ministry to help talk about, yes, the mission statement, but also what's working well within the mission, what support do they need from the parish staff, do they have a plan of succession for when the time comes to move on, etc.

The talented lay professionals at these parishes maintain a good, cooperative relationship with and offer accountability to pastors; their contributions in turn spark new initiatives with direction, vision, purpose, and goals. Fr. Paul Manning of St. Paul Inside the Walls in Madison, New Jersey, used words such as "genuine," "supportive," "honest," and "wonderful" to describe his staff. Pastors appreciate colleagues who share with them honest ideas and opinions about decisions they make. One pastor told us his staff makes him look good. A pastor in the Northeast remarked, "I would say, first, that we have a wonderful staff, faithful to the Gospel and to the Church, who are able to communicate that faithfulness in contemporary and relevant ways, and who, most importantly, live that faithfulness out in their daily lives." The depth and breadth of these roles highlighted by pastors show the invaluable impact strong lay leadership is having on the life of the Church today.

GUARDING THE PASTOR'S TIME AND WELL-BEING

The number of lay ministers teaming up with pastors to lead parishes today is an inspiration. In order to develop a strong team, these pastors prioritize the need to invite, train, and empower talented leaders to assume vital roles in parish leadership. But once the lay staff is in place, the pastor must be willing to trust that the responsibilities assigned to team members will be handled and allow the laity to do their work. Only then can he devote himself to the elements of parish leadership exclusive to his role as the leader of leaders. Only then will he have the time, energy, and vision necessary to do these things well (see figure 1.2).

Pastor self-care is crucial to the long-term vitality of strong leadership, and pastors who are leading well understand its importance. A pastor must allow himself time to pray, regroup, rest, and relax in order to remain at the top of his game. More than 70 percent of the pastors we interviewed described positive self-care habits that nourish their spirituality, maintain their health, and help them enjoy free time. When we asked Fr. Jeremy Leatherby of Presentation of the Blessed Virgin Mary parish in Sacramento, California, what he does to keep himself going, he responded, "I exercise. I try to stay in good

Figure 1.2 Disciplined delegation

health. For free time—leisure time—I like to read. I find [reading] very relaxing, very recreational."

Exercise ranged from golf course and gym visits to downhill skiing and dance lessons. Hobbies included gardening, reading, and art. Traveling was a popular choice for spending free time. Time taken away from day-to-day responsibilities allows for introspection, as Fr. Fred Bailey of Santa Clara de Assisi in Yorba Linda, California, told us: "I'm highly comfortable traveling by myself, dining for hours with my book and food and just thinking and pondering and experiencing quiet stillness. So I take my time away. I have a cabin in the mountains, and I do that regularly—if not every week, every other week." These times of stillness often make room for deeper, more contemplative prayer.

Our priests make private prayer a priority. Many pray every morning, every night, and in between to remain faithful to their office. Days rarely go by without at least one Mass; sometimes they celebrate as many as four. Msgr. John Barry of American Martyrs parish in Manhattan Beach, California, described himself as a bee hopping from flower to flower for prayer. Some pastors find benefit in meeting regularly with lay groups for prayer, which can mean simply getting together one evening per week to spend time in discussion and prayer about ministry and the state of the parish. Other pastors have a priest support group on which they rely.

PRIEST SUPPORT GROUPS

The fifty-one pastors[6] (one in five) who mentioned spiritual directors or priest support groups did so spontaneously, and they reported that the relationships were meaningful and essential to their well-being. Composed entirely of priests, some of the support groups mentioned by our pastors have been meeting for more than thirty years. They fill an important need in the lives of their members. They provide a space where priests can gain perspective and talk to others who are in a unique position to understand their hopes and challenges. These groups can be as small as a pair of individuals, as is the case for Fr. John Bergstadt of St. John the Baptist parish in Green Bay,

Wisconsin: "I've been active in a priest support group almost from the beginning of my priesthood. I have a close friend. We talk each night on the phone and share some of the stories, talk about some of the crazy things, and then I feel better and go to bed. In the first couple years, because of the building project and everything else, I didn't spend too much time doing it. You can work real hard for a while, but you can't do that forever."

More commonly, these priest support groups consist of six to eight priests. They meet as frequently as weekly or as seldom as once every six weeks. Fr. Bill Stenzel of St. Mary of Celle parish in Berwyn, Illinois, said his group has a daily conversation where they can simply vent to people in their same line of work: "We're all in the same boat, working for the same outfit. It has created some blessings, and it has all the challenges of the current day."

Fr. Kerry Beaulieu of Our Lady Queen of Angels in Newport Beach, California, pinpointed just how helpful these priest support group sessions can be: "It's mainly social, but it almost always includes some aspect of sharing about the experience of ministry and life and work that's going on right now. Our group just met last Friday, and one of the guys had a sister who just came down with cancer, so we shared a lot about that. We talk about our stresses and our strains, and it's an opportunity to vent and release some of that pressure."

Priests are human beings who need the support of friends, family, and community just like everyone else. These days, when anxiety or stress becomes a problem, priests can also seek professional counseling without suffering the stigma once attached to such a course of action. When leading becomes a challenge, support groups help priests maintain their stamina and vision for the inspiring, but somewhat overwhelming, reality that is priesthood.

CRUCIAL TAKEAWAYS

1. Pope Francis is positively modeling shared leadership to our pastors: one in three of them spontaneously mentioned his influence during our interviews.

2. Shared leadership—practiced in various ways—is the optimal model of parish leadership.

3. Vibrant parishes take pride in their strong, professional staffs and programs for volunteer leadership. Sixty-seven percent of our pastors named lay leaders as a major parish asset.

4. More than 70 percent of our pastors described positive self-care habits. They are disciplined about prayer and exercise, participate in priest support groups, and in general, protect time for their indispensable roles as pastors.

2
—

CHALLENGES OF
SHARED LEADERSHIP

I don't know how you create leaders, and that is a struggle. You can give the ideas to people, but they have to have the fire in the belly to do it. The ideas can be clear and they can read the books and so on, but how do you create leaders?

—Fr. Tracy O'Sullivan
St. Raphael, Los Angeles, California

Despite the rosy picture painted in the last chapter of well-coordinated parish staffs, even the successful pastors we surveyed spoke of problems with personnel. In fact, nearly half (45.2 percent) spoke of challenges they face related to working with some of their staff members. Some of those interactions are difficult enough to keep 28 percent of our pastors up at night. And the busyness of building an effective staff can distract a pastor from finding and developing new parish leaders.

Complicating this equation is the inevitability that most pastors will be reassigned away from the parishes they currently serve. Whatever long-term initiatives they and their leadership teams establish, in the end, it will be up to their successors to support or abandon them. Finally, the priest shortage facing the Catholic Church compounds these leadership challenges. With fewer and fewer pastors in

American Catholic parishes, it is no surprise that these pastors ruminate on parish leadership problems.

"What keeps you up at night?" was one question in our interview protocol. The most common answer we heard—given by roughly 30 percent of our pastors—was "Nothing, I sleep very well!"[1] But when pastors do lie awake at night, they most frequently worry about interpersonal tensions and finances (see figure 2.1).

Figure 2.1 Priestly concerns

RESPONSES RECIEVED TO THE QUESTION: "WHAT KEEPS YOU UP AT NIGHT?"

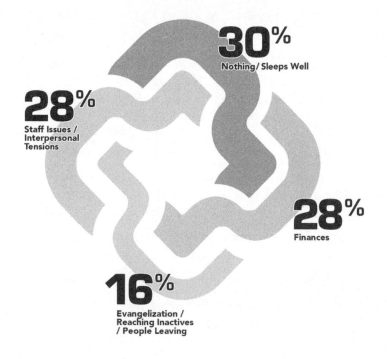

30%
Nothing/ Sleeps Well

28%
Staff Issues /
Interpersonal
Tensions

28%
Finances

16%
Evangelization /
Reaching Inactives
/ People Leaving

N = 201 (THIS QUESTION WAS ADDED AFTER SOME OF THE INTERVIEWS HAD ALREADY TAKEN PLACE)
PASTORS COULD GIVE MORE THAN ONE ANSWER, SO RESPONSES DO NOT TOTAL 100%

Even though the majority of pastors (80.3 percent) in our study named leadership as a source of pride and strength in their parish, more than one in four (28.0 percent) saw opportunities for growth or change in staffing, and, again, almost half (45.2 percent) considered staffing to be a challenge. The takeaway is this: eight out of ten pastors talked about strong leadership while at the same time seven out of ten (73.2 percent) admitted to being challenged or at least recognizing room for improvement within their staffs. Church staffs and staffing are pervasive challenges in Catholic parishes.

Slightly more than a third of our pastors (35.6 percent) considered finances both a strength and a challenge. This makes sense when we consider that parishes, by definition, live from year to year, only rarely running surpluses. They are, in essence, only as solvent as the last capital campaign. There are virtually no endowments. Even in communities with affluent parishioners, strong vision and leadership is required to ensure generous giving, successful campaigns, and a balanced budget. The biggest worries, then, were interpersonal tensions and finances, both of which are staffing concerns.

MAINTAINING STAFF HARMONY

Parishes can be plagued by petty tensions among staff members. Staff members may have difficult personalities to manage (e.g., dominating, insecure, disorganized). As a pastor from an urban parish in the South told us, "It can be really stressful managing the people who are hurt and angry and want to lash out. Or it's hard managing if an individual has a hero complex and wants to take on the bishop."

The tendency to avoid confrontation was a thread that ran through pastor comments about staff challenges. Pastors can be determined to make the pieces fit together despite the difficulties. A pastor from the Eastern Seaboard told of a time he ignored a staff consensus to fire an employee. Even after years of trying to help the individual work well in some capacity, while fielding more comments from staff members about their inability to work well as a team, the pastor pressed on. Finally, after four years he fired the staff member; he said he would never wait that long again.

Other pastors said they are "not good at conflict," that they "wouldn't complain if [a staff member] quit," or that "a broken relationship is so difficult for me." A pastor in a Midwestern suburb had this to say regarding anxiety over confronting difficult employees: "The thing that keeps me awake is if I need to be particularly firm with someone and know that I have to have that meeting with them. It's sometimes difficult to know how to walk that line." These challenges drain pastors of energy and initiative.

Contentious, opinionated, traumatized, terrorized, and *territorial* were words used to describe staff members. A pastor with a competent and sensitive human resources person on staff has support when he must handle a difficult staff interaction, but even with support, the final difficult decisions and conversations generally must come from the pastor himself.

DISCERNING LAY POTENTIAL

When a person's strengths and talents are matched to the role he or she assumes, greater efficiency and harmony exists in an organization. It is imperative to take the time to place the right volunteer or staff person in the role and not just quickly fill a need.

Fr. Michael Saporito of the Parish Community of St. Helen in Westfield, New Jersey, was one pastor who defined this issue: "We have the gifts and talents sitting in our pews to help us to make that happen. I know it's here. It just needs to be called forth. And so the question is, how do you do that? The opportunity is there for us. We've got people who would say, 'Tell me how, show me what you want me to do, lead us.'"

To answer his question, there are many different approaches to proactively discerning lay talent as opposed to waiting for parishioners to come forward who may or may not be a good fit for a staff or volunteer position. Gallup's StrengthsFinder[2] survey is one of several tools available to pastors to help identify the strengths and talents of the people already on staff as well as those in the pews.

For some parishes, a stewardship coordinator takes on the task of discernment. Acting as a bridge between parish needs and the talents of the parishioners, this individual meets with families registered at the parish and helps them become more engaged in parish life. Pastors with stewardship coordinators in their parishes started by finding someone with the right personality, energy, and expertise to talk with leaders and parishioners about their interests and skills and match them with appropriate projects and tasks.

Fr. Terence Keehan of Holy Family parish in Inverness, Illinois, asks his parishioners, "What are you good at, what gifts do you have, what do you need to develop more, and then how do you make choices to put yourself in a position where you're going to express those gifts and talents with the world to make the world a better place?" However talent is discerned, the important thing is to place people in parish roles that align needs of the parish with gifts of the ministers.

Helping people discover their strengths and how to use them can have a resounding effect on parish life overall. Fr. Jack Walmesly of Our Lady of Guadalupe in Seattle, Washington, said his parish once had an inferiority complex with respect to a wealthier, more robust parish not far from theirs: "I would say the parish has grown in its confidence as a parish, and it recognizes that there are real leaders here. There are real folks who can lead, who can move the ball forward, who can plan, who can participate." Talented leaders were identified, and they stepped forward. With that, the self-confidence of the whole parish picked up.

Parishes have creative, talented, and energetic individuals in their pews. Providing these people with tools to help them clarify and discern those talents is in itself a way of welcoming them to deeper engagement and spirituality. Their using of their talents also makes it much more likely that their first steps into ministry will be highly successful.

VOLUNTEERS

Not all leadership is professional or requires wages. Building up leadership capabilities within the parish may require a change in mindset among the staff and parishioners. During our interviews, numerous pastors expressed a desire to help their parishioners see their primary role in ministry as disciple making, no matter what that ministry was. They want to develop leaders who see their work in the Church first as a way to bring others into a deeper relationship with Christ and second as a specific ministry.

Pastors have a profound power to inspire and encourage individuals to deeper discipleship and deeper service to their parish. For some of our pastors, the initial step to growing disciple-making leaders in their communities begins with identifying the gifts and talents of their parishioners. The next step is to channel those gifts into leadership opportunities that use those talents. Warren Bennis, scholar and organizational consultant, is famous for saying, "Becoming a leader is synonymous with becoming yourself. It is precisely that simple, and it is also that difficult."[3] But Bennis also states that "it is the capacity to develop and improve their skills that distinguishes leaders from followers."[4] As people's talents grow and are used in parish life, their commitment to what they are doing evolves as does their own discipleship.

Many pastors described this phenomenon in their parishes. One gave the example of an IT professional who never realized that the technological savvy he honed at work could be his donation to the Church; he entered ministry in his parish and developed into teaching RCIA. Another pastor had a parish full of people who were willing to clean and cook but just required the extra push from him to develop their own ministries in this area.

Ron Ryan, pastoral coordinator for St. Anne Church in Seattle, Washington, saw shared responsibility as a big step in drawing parishioners into parish leadership: "My focus is trying to help the laypeople of the parish buy into ownership, for lack of a better term. So I really focus on trying to help the vision come from them, rather than through me. Rather than looking simply to the priest or the pastoral leader, I think that helps to engage more and more members of the parish."

For Fr. Damien Cook, pastor of St. Peter in Omaha, Nebraska, this deepening of lay leaders' involvement came unexpectedly. "I have families who come early and give out books to people and say 'Hi, how are you?' and 'Where are you from?' So I don't even have a plan of scheduled greeters. People just do it because they see a need and they want people to feel welcome." The greeters at his parish are discipling as well as welcoming. The deepening happened organically because of the encouraging environment at this parish.

Another approach to developing disciple-making ministers is encouraging them to reach out beyond the parish. Fr. Xavier Lavagetto, O.P., pastor of St. Dominic parish in San Francisco, California, put it this way: "Really speaking to people and inviting people—we gotta go out there and start. It's wrong for the Church to wait for people to come to us. The only way we can do that is through the laity—so, lay ministry, lay ministry, lay ministry—and really empowering our laypeople. And I'll tell you—they're the word of mouth that attracts. They're the word of mouth that gets us sixty people in RCIA."

Fr. Michael Meyers of St. James Church in Redondo Beach, California, described how ministry leaders at his parish continually reach out to invite new people. This means he never looks for new sacristans, new lectors, or new Eucharistic Ministers. They are constantly brought in, developed, and trained, and they fit in. The ministries are organized enough to operate on their own without the pastor having to do anything for them.

HIRING AND PAYING LAY PROFESSIONALS

A thriving church community relies on numerous parishioners to do the work of the parish. Therefore, the pastor must focus special attention on developing and hiring staff with leadership skills and pastoral experience to oversee the good work being done. This requires that a parish pay wages that will attract effective leaders.

Hiring and compensation are two sources of the financial concerns that keep 28 percent of our pastors up at night. Though only 11 percent of those pastors identified hiring and compensation as the sources of their concerns, patterns that emerged from their comments are worth reviewing.

For instance, a parish may be faced with a dilemma such as this: There is only enough money in the budget to add one new staff member. This will not provide enough coverage for the work that needs to be done. The parish receives a small number of applicants, none of whom is truly outstanding. The post either remains vacant or is staffed by someone who is a less-than-ideal fit. The hiring problem can be self-reinforcing. The paid positions available for qualified candidates either offer poor compensation or are located in places where few trained ministers looking for work may live. So parishes hire low-wage earning, underqualified personnel (see figure 2.2).

Figure 2.2 You get what you pay for

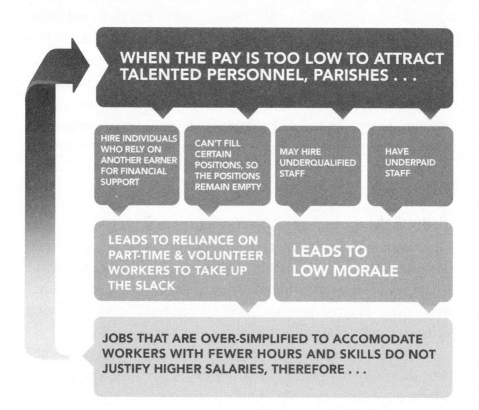

The following remark from Fr. Thomas Santen of St. Joseph parish in Manchester, Missouri, illuminates the critical problem related to lay leadership: "The declining number of clergy and the fact that [the] leadership of the Church has not put very much energy into the development of lay leadership are deep concerns because I think the viability of this parish right now is going to be tied to strong lay leaders."

In 2011 the Emerging Models of Pastoral Leadership project estimated that the US Church is adding about 790 new lay ecclesial ministers to parish ministry staffs each year and projected that the trend would continue through 2015.[5] Likewise, CARA found that the number of lay ministers nationwide increased between 2005 and 2015.[6] But several pastors in our dataset reported great difficulty in finding qualified people to fill open positions in their parish.

Fr. Thomas Belleque of St. Louis parish in Bellevue, Washington, spoke about this issue: "We've had a few hiring processes recently for open positions, and I was dismayed at either the lack of folks who applied or the lack of qualifications I found in the folks who did apply. And so I think that's going to be a real concern for our career ministers as well. Are we supporting and training and encouraging folks to serve our communities?"

Salaries for lay professional ministry are generally low. CARA reports that 47 percent of lay ecclesial ministers are involved in ministry in more than one parish and 20 percent of them have additional paid jobs outside of ministry.[7] Fr. Paul White of Church of Holy Apostles in McHenry, Illinois, shared his concerns: "We've lost a lot of lay ministers, professional lay ministers, and we haven't thought about what we're going to do in the future. Young people go to colleges that cost $40,000 a year, and then come out, and then cannot work in the Church unless their parents are loaded."

Msgr. Vincent Rush of Our Lady of Grace parish in West Babylon, New York, believes the excitement of the Second Vatican Council drove educated people, some with graduate degrees, to pursue a career in the Church despite the pay being lower. He elaborated that many of these individuals relied on their spouses for the primary financial support for their families; however, since the economic crisis of 2008, the working conditions in the Church no longer offer a viable career path for younger people. The goal is to find the right people and pay them well, but the reality of the personnel spiral indicated in figure 2.2 provides little incentive for people to choose lay ministry as a career.

Even when parishes can find talented ministers to hire, they often must help them develop leadership skills. As Fr. Chris Michelson of St. Albert the Great parish in Knoxville, Tennessee, said, "Empowering people to use their gifts and talents is a real challenge here—only because of the education level and being in roles that they're not used to, being leaders. That's probably our biggest challenge—just empowering people and teaching them how to be leaders and how to lead others."

STALE LAY LEADERSHIP

Discerning what is the best course of action when a paid or volunteer leader is simply not meeting expectations is a significant challenge to pastors and their senior staffs in many of the parishes of our study. Several of our pastors talked about current situations in their parishes where someone who has been in a position for many years has lost the creative interest required to keep the ministry alive and dynamic. This was a sensitive, frustrating topic for them.

One pastor told us, "We have three small communities that have had the same leader for well over ten years, and you recognize how those communities are not as vibrant and alive as other communities who've made a shared leadership model much more conducive to involving members of that small faith community—and [that community is] growing."

It is difficult to fire a professional staff person or a volunteer, but sometimes that needs to be done for the sake of the wider community and growth of the parish.

DEVELOPING LAY LEADERSHIP

Leaders are trusted and respected, both for what they do and who they are—for their competence and their character. This points back to the importance of putting the right person in the right job. "It's all leadership," said Fr. Tracy O'Sullivan of St. Raphael Church in Los Angeles, California. "That's the issue in the parish and the school. That's the Catholic system. After many years of observing this struggle, [I see it as] the key issue: How do you pinpoint leaders? How do you get them and place them in the right place and give them the support that they need and let them blossom?"

Once a parish has identified leaders, the leadership development process has only begun. To maintain the momentum and develop leaders successfully, it is essential to have a plan in place. One part of that plan needs to be the ongoing mentorship and development of current leaders. The other is the development of future leaders—what is sometimes called a "leadership pipeline," a system for continued recruiting of new leaders and the advancement and training of current leaders into more responsible positions. Pastors we spoke to are always searching for leadership development and training support.

Leadership training has been available in the public sector for many years. In the Catholic world, several opportunities have developed in recent years.[8] Through them, pastors have access to leadership development techniques.

CATHOLIC MODELS

Since 1990, Catholic Leadership Institute (CLI) has offered training, often through consultants, not just for priests but also for deacons and parish and diocesan leaders. Fr. Michael G. Ryan of St. James Cathedral in Seattle, Washington, described his experience with CLI this way: "We spent quite a lot of time this summer trying to revise how we work together as a pastoral team, a group of fifteen which includes myself and fourteen lay ecclesial ministers. We brought in an outside consultant who spent a good amount of time listening to each person and what the problems and the successes of the group were and how we can do better. I learned a lot and so did [the rest of our leaders]."

Useful outside perspectives such as these broaden a pastor's vision for the parish's true leadership needs. Another pastor we spoke to sent his leadership team to CLI's *Tending the Talents* program—eleven days of training to help leaders sharpen their individual talents—and was entirely satisfied with the results.

Christ Renews His Parish (CRHP) is a program that has helped parishes since 1969. Since more than one thousand parishes have used the CRHP program, it was no surprise that some of them were in our dataset. Speaking about a CRHP hybrid retreat program, Fr. Michael Saporito of the Parish Community of St. Helen in Westfield, New Jersey, explained the impact it had on his parish over time: "This will be our twenty-fifth year of that overnight retreat, and it has really catapulted the many ministries, lay involvement, and laypeople coming forward to be involved in our community."

Two other fine examples of Catholic leadership development tools are Amazing Parish and Cornerstone. Amazing Parish, formed by philanthropist John Martin and noted author Patrick Lencioni, convenes parish teams to hear important speakers and meet one another. Cornerstone is another program that a number of our pastors spoke of with great respect. It offers annual retreats for men and women in parishes or among groups of parishes. Cornerstone's goal is for participants to develop a stronger connection to God and to live the life that God wants for them.

EVANGELICAL AND CORPORATE MODELS

Pastors we spoke with also made use of leadership development initiatives that were not specifically Catholic. Many of our pastors were open to ecumenical influences in the area of leadership development just as they were in the area of homiletics.

Prominent evangelical pastors including Rick Warren, Bill Hybels, and Andy Stanley offer materials for leadership development programs. "I am a good copier," Fr. Tom Connery of St. Peter Church in DeLand, Florida, joked, reflecting how deliberate pastors are about using proven leadership initiatives wherever they come from.

Another way our pastors initiated leadership development was by revising outside materials for use in a parish setting. Msgr. Paul Dudziak of St. Stephen Martyr parish in Washington, DC, leveraged a program he taught in a graduate-school course to suit the needs of his parish: "My methodology was adult educational methodology, meaning a variety of methodologies, structured experiences, feedback instruments, role play, case study, brief lectures. . . ." Another parish developed its own leadership program with the help of a female minister from a local Protestant church who had expertise in leadership development in the corporate world.

Some parishes used more than one initiative to develop their leaders. After reading *The Seven Habits of Highly Effective People* by Stephen Covey five times while in the seminary, Fr. John Jirak of Blessed Sacrament parish in Wichita, Kansas, incorporated the lessons from the book into leadership initiatives and later combined them with insights gleaned from a leadership center that his state provided: "We've taken these leadership retreats with our staff, teachers, and lay leaders. We've taken our nine people on our staff to a one-year secular leadership program. Then, every week at our staff meetings, we spend fifteen to twenty minutes on leadership formation, where we work with the principles and competencies that we learned in the leadership program. I'm a big believer that there [are] a lot of good leadership programs out there." He said his view on leadership had shifted; he no longer thought of leadership as a position but as an activity that anyone can practice anywhere at any time.

HOMEGROWN MODELS

When looking at leadership development, it is important to remember that every parish is at a unique stage of growth, which will require different leadership strategies at different times. As a result, we found that instead of making use of the various development programs currently available to them, occasionally our pastors dealt with problems and concerns in a more organic fashion. "It's really important that I try to connect with folks where they are and where they're coming from because my white suburban upbringing doesn't equip me, necessarily, to understand or meet them where they are," said Fr. William Thaden from Sacred Heart Chapel in Lorain, Ohio. He favors a more organic leadership approach where his leadership team naturally fills in the gaps rather than using a more structured training method. "What doesn't work here is the corporate mindset," Fr. Thaden explained.

> If there's a ministry that's flourishing, the last thing you want to do is try to put it under a structure or commission or something. It's more organic: Where's the energy for this coming from? What do I need to affirm? What needs to be challenged or stretched? There's a lot of ownership here, either because the things they're doing have to do with their culture or because they built this parish with their hands and it's theirs. I can't come in from some side angle and say, "Here's what we're doing." I've really got to know what's motivating them and what their feeling is on things.

This pastor's perspective of drilling down to find out what kinds of leadership work at any given moment is indicative of a more organic leadership development plan.

His parish is also an example (frankly, a rare one in our data) of a situation in which organizational management solutions were not right for a parish. It offers hope via an alternative route: if a parish has set up structures and committees and is still flagging, it might be that they need less structure, not more. It is an alternative leadership development model for a parish that has tried structure and wonders, "Why isn't this working? What are we doing wrong?"

NAVIGATING PASTOR TRANSITIONS

It has been said that great leaders are always working themselves out of a job. They are always on the lookout for who is to take up the reins once they are gone. Parishes that have learned to develop a culture of continual invitation to leadership, training, and growth in responsibility for their members are predisposed to ongoing health and growth when pastor transitions occur.

Given the importance of leadership, can parishes thrive through transitions or periods of poor leadership? Times of change are always on the horizon. They may be far in the distance, but they are coming.

In 1983 the United States Conference of Catholic Bishops approved complementary legislation for canon 522, decreeing that "individual ordinaries may appoint pastors to a six-year term of office. The possibility of renewing their terms is left to the discretion of the diocesan bishop. The primary provision of Canon 522, that pastors may be appointed for an indefinite period of time, remains in force." At the time of our interviews, pastors in our database had pastored their current parishes for anywhere from one to thirty-nine years. Pastor transitions were on the minds of many of them; the topic came up in exactly half (50 percent) of our interviews.

Although parishes are spiritual places that differ greatly from corporate environments, a comparison to the corporate world can be useful when considering continuity of leadership. The chief executive officer of General Electric generally spends the last two years of tenure vetting possible replacement candidates. Similarly, pastors might be well advised to spend time considering their parish's current and future transitions while ensuring that they surround themselves with the best leadership teams available.

An upcoming pastor transition can be a source of tremendous stress, but it can also spur organizational planning and leadership development initiatives within the parish. Fr. Douglas Doussan of St. Gabriel the Archangel in New Orleans, Louisiana, is someone who has taken a particularly systematic approach to getting his parish ready for future transitions:

> I'm seventy-nine. I told them that I have no plans to retire, but I never know when I'm going to get sick or die or have to retire for some reason, and so it's very important that our present leadership have adequate training in spirituality, in Vatican II theology, and in pastoral skills. So we preached on this; we recruited our parish leaders, so we've had a program. It's a six-month program; it's one Saturday from three and a half to four hours. We started it back in October. In June will be our sixth and last session. And we did an

hour last time on spirituality, an hour on Vatican II theology (the major documents), an hour on pastoral skills. And we've had seventy-five people participate.

But succession is something some pastors intentionally avoid thinking about altogether. "I am careful not to look into the future and feel that I'm responsible for that," said Msgr. John Barry of American Martyrs parish in Manhattan Beach, California. "I will trust that when I step aside, there will be someone who will come here, who will be able to serve the people, and who will bring new ideas and new vision." Fr. Paul White of Church of Holy Apostles in McHenry, Illinois, distanced himself from the idea that the parish "belongs" to him. "I keep telling my people, 'This is not my parish,'" he said. "I'm here for the time I'm here. I can be moved. This is not my parish. It's their parish. My job is to do what I can while I'm here, what I envision, and make sure everybody's being heard and we're going in the right direction."

The reality is that a priest may be called upon to serve at another parish at any time. Fr. Adan Sandoval of Our Lady of the Mount parish in Cicero, Illinois, remarked, "The biggest challenge that I can encounter in the future [is that] I have to go and take another place and my parish will not have enough leadership people to take over. We are working tirelessly to form the laypeople through liturgy, through leadership, but at the same time, that would be a big thing that might happen."

Fr. Michael Ryan of St. James Cathedral in Seattle, Washington, emphasized how important a parish's dialogue with their diocese needs to be during that time. "At some point I'm going to step aside here," he said. "I think there will be a significant challenge to find a way to do the leadership succession that's not going to somehow throw the place into a tailspin. And I hope the diocese is wise enough to work with us on that and do it in a way that will really help us move into a transition of leadership."

Fr. Tony Zimmer of St. Anthony on the Lake parish in Pewaukee, Wisconsin, shared similar concerns about his vision collapsing when he leaves, but he devised a succession plan to safeguard the leadership strides made. He told us of a retreat his parish designed specifically to prepare lay leaders to shoulder more of the parish leadership in the hope of making pastoral transition less difficult: "On this retreat, and the Confirmation retreats, we step back. We've empowered them so much that they basically run it. We're there to guide them, support them, but we let them lead the prayers, we let them do the ministry and give the talks and the testimonials. It's an empowerment."

Some parishes with strong parishioner participation and support have an uncanny ability to make things work regardless of who is pastoring the community. Prior to Fr. Rob Cook's arrival, Sacred Heart church in Boise, Idaho, had not had a resident priest for nine years, but that did not deter parishioners: "For three years, a religious sister was the parish life director. After her, a deacon took charge for six years, and parish life was very good. During these times, a retired priest or a priest parochial vicar were present for sacramental purposes."

As pastors are expected to care for the members of their congregation, part of the ministry of the laity includes caring for the needs of the pastors who serve them. One method some parishes have used to build the relationship between the new pastor and lay leaders is to create a transition team made up of parishioners whose mandate is to smooth the pastoral transition by providing insight, advice, and support to the pastor through his first year of ministry in a new parish.

A parish that has developed a system for continually bringing new people into parish leadership and advancing them in responsibility and ministerial involvement is prepared for the dynamics of parish life and will likely navigate transitions more smoothly, whether a transition to a new pastor or the departure of a current staff member.

Parishes with outgoing pastors need to be ready to use their transitional time as an opportunity to rely on lay leadership regardless of the pastor in place. For instance, pastors spoke optimistically about assembling a new pastoral council, working with an incoming office manager, finding space in the budget for a full-time music director, or updating job descriptions or performance-evaluation processes.

Staff changes can provide opportunities for parishes to evolve. This was the case for Fr. Bob Stec at St. Ambrose parish in Brunswick, Ohio. "We had a staff change, which opened up a whole new door of possibility for us that wasn't there a year or two ago." Pastors alluded to hiring such lay leaders as youth ministers, campus ministers, parochial vicars, and new school principals during times of transition. Fr. Stec continued to speak of transitional hires: "If we looked at the two-year plan, do we turn down what we believe is a really good step forward? No, so, it's better that we take these shorter year, year-and-a-half, two-year looks, so that we can be more responsive and make better use of what's available at a given time."

TRANSITION DIFFICULTIES

When a new pastor arrives, his first function is building relationships with the staff and his new parishioners. Some pastors are known to bring staff members along with them to a new parish, which adds to the adjustment. A pastor from the South talked about the difficulty he experienced blending new and old staff members: "There were people that I was able to acquire and then there were the folks that have been here, and I've never been able to bring those two groups together. That's been my failure. So I just think, at night . . . if we were all on the same bus and going in the same direction and had a good, fun relationship with each other that we enjoyed . . . and looked forward to working together, all of us together—goodness gracious, it could have been so much better."

Even when a parish is lucky enough to have a good pastor and the community thrives under his leadership, not all leadership problems are solved. In fact, when a pastor is the embodiment of a good leader, questions arise about how the parish will sustain its energy after he leaves. Will the same pastor be as effective if he starts having to rotate from one parish to another because of the priest shortage? If the pastor sets the tone, how can parishes thrive when the incoming pastor is not a strong leader?

Transitioning the leadership of a parish from one pastor with leadership qualities to another without them is a problem that frustrates parish progress. Said one pastor from the Northeast:

> We've also had really bad personnel policies [at the diocesan level]. Promising initiatives are not studied as best practices and possibly emulated. Let's say a pastor transfers—[promising initiatives] get cut off at the head because it's time for somebody to move. There's very little thought in trying to find out what's successful and find somebody who will be a good fit with continuing that success. The first parish I served in would be a perfect example of that. We had a visionary pastor, a good staff, and when it came time for him to retire, the person who replaced him was a good human being but didn't have anything like the vision. I don't think it was intentional, but it dismantled the life of the parish.

For this pastor, and many like him, uncertainty looms without a transitional leadership model on which to rely.

A time of transition can be seen as an opportunity for a parish to reevaluate leadership positions, how they lead, and in what direction they are heading. Whether a parish is currently facing transition or trying to develop a system for ongoing leadership development, both situations open the door to look at evaluation of staff and reevaluation of ministries. Msgr. Francis Malone of Christ the King parish in Little Rock, Arkansas, used his transition into a new parish as an opportunity for staff evaluation:

> I ask them to first of all give me an up-to-date job description: anything that might have changed over the past year, anything that was added to their responsibilities, anything they undertook that now they are doing on a regular basis. So I get to see what they're doing and the job description, then to see how they view themselves, and then, depending on their answers,

whether I will need to give them a charge for the next year. That's the opportunity. I get the opportunity to evaluate them and see what's going on for the next year, and I choose to do that privately with them.

CONFRONTING THE PRIEST SHORTAGE

As indicated in figure 2.3, the "supply" of priests in the United States continues to decline while "demand" grows, in the form of a growing Catholic population. Increasing numbers of parishes do not have their own pastor; of the 17,337 Catholic parishes in the United States in 2015, 3,533 did not have a resident pastor, which equates to nearly one in five.[9] In 2035, it is estimated that there will be only 12,520 diocesan priests active in ministry in the United States, representing a 34.5 percent decline from 2010.[10]

The dwindling number of diocesan priests is a major source of concern for even the most vibrant parishes in the country. It is a difficult topic to talk about. "We won't have to worry about closing parishes. They'll close on their own, and it won't just be people [leaving] the pews," said Fr. Joseph Ring of Christ the King in Springfield, Illinois. "We hardly have priests at the altar." Another pastor, on the West Coast, voiced concerns about how the Church will respond to the vocation crisis. At fifty-five, he is well below the median age in his archdiocese, which leaves him wondering what the American Catholic parish will look like in the future. Msgr. Robert Yeazel, across the country at Holy Cross parish in Dewitt, New York, worries about the seismic effects the shortage will have on spirituality: "We sometimes can't fill parishes, and—the vocation crisis is the main driver right now—we still try to entice young men to go into the seminary or young women to the convent but it's very difficult today. We have two seminarians here now, but it's very difficult. And that keeps me up because I have the feeling that when we're gone, the shortage is really going to affect the spirituality of our people."

The decline over the last fifty years in the number of priests has contributed to the growth in size of the average parish. The number of

Figure 2.3 Number of priests

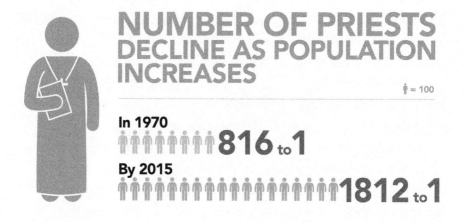

NUMBER OF PRIESTS DECLINE AS POPULATION INCREASES

♀ = 100

In 1970
♀♀♀♀♀♀♀♀**816 to 1**

By 2015
♀♀♀♀♀♀♀♀♀♀♀♀♀♀♀♀♀♀**1812 to 1**

Catholic parishes in the United States as of 2015 (17,337) is the smallest number since 1965, when there were a similar number (17,637). The current total shows a marked decline since 1990, when the total number peaked at 19,620.[11] Since then, the number of parishes in the United States has declined by about 11.6 percent—a net loss of 2,283 parishes in the last twenty-four years.

MERGED PARISHES

There are many ways that parish populations are being redistributed, one of which is the reassigning of a territory. After a parish closes, it can be the case that its congregation or, more specifically, the territory they reside in is reassigned to another parish. Overnight, people effectively become members of another parish. Other times, two smaller parishes will merge at the site of one parish. This happened on a large scale in the Archdiocese of New York in November 2014, when Cardinal Timothy M. Dolan announced that fifty New York parishes would be merged with others. These mergers contribute to the parish "supersizing" effect.[12]

Mergers are taking place in the East at the same time as newer and larger parishes are under construction in the South and West, where the Catholic population is still experiencing considerable growth.

These two trends are responsible for what are called "million dollar parishes."[13] Twenty-eight percent of Catholic parishes in the United States now have annual revenue in excess of $1 million.[14] A handful of these parishes have upwards of twenty thousand parishioners; their administration could be likened to that of a small corporation.

Fr. William Konicki of Sacred Heart of Jesus parish in Hopedale, Massachusetts, recognizes that his parish is not far from a pair of huge churches: "They can just add a Mass and take us in. I think one of our challenges is to help people realize that we need to stay an active, involved community and not be afraid of closing."

For others, the supply problem extends well beyond priests. "I see the shortage not only with priests but also with qualified ministers because we're such a rural parish," said Fr. Steven Verhelst of St. Mary parish in Willmar, Minnesota. "It's hard to get people, just like in the medical profession, to come out into the rural areas and to serve. I see that dwindling of resources. That concerns me because the needs are still as great as ever."

CHALLENGES RECAPPED

1. Staff harmony can be an ongoing challenge that impedes parish vitality and growth.

2. The pool of lay applicants may not be adequate to meet the need for qualified, gifted lay leaders, in part because of low pay rates.

3. Lay leaders require ongoing training and development opportunities.

4. A smooth transition from one pastor to the next demands prudent planning on the part of the departing pastor and leadership team and careful discernment by diocesan leaders.

5. The decreasing number of priests available for parish leadership, coupled with increasing numbers of Catholics, requires new models of leadership and careful, honest strategic planning.

PART II

GREAT PARISHES FOSTER SPIRITUAL MATURITY AND PLAN FOR DISCIPLESHIP

A HEART FOR JESUS

I have a friend who likes to say that the mind is a good servant but a terrible master. This is partly because we tend to overthink and rationalize, but it is also because when we rely on our intellects we often give short shrift to our spiritual lives. I think it is fair to say that my mind has been the ringmaster for most of my life and that, while I have tried to live honorably, my focus until recent years was far removed from spiritual pursuits.

With age, I seem to have developed more of a heart for Jesus. Maybe it's because I have fewer distractions now that my children have left the nest and my business life has become less frenetic. Maybe it's the grace of hindsight, having walked far enough down the road of my spiritual journey to be able to look back and recognize that my faith—my heart for Jesus—was there all along and has kept me centered. Two things are for sure: Jesus is faithful, and he has promised that if we seek him, we will eventually find him. My spiritual journey has certainly not been along a straight line from point A to point B.

It hasn't always moved at the same pace. But, mercifully, I have kept moving forward surely, if slowly, and the pace has quickened as I've gotten older.

I have always lived passionately, throwing myself into whatever task was at hand. But the compulsion I once felt to succeed in business, in politics, or in whatever was my top priority at the moment has given way to a compelling desire to know the will and mind of God and to follow it.

As a result, somewhat to my surprise, I find I am no longer reluctant or embarrassed to speak publicly about my faith. Moreover, I have a growing enjoyment of others who share our common Christianity, finding faith a much more important common denominator than those I used to look for. I am trying to reorder my priorities and obligations to leave plenty of time for spiritual reflection, prayer, and service to the Church. Too often I honor this desire in the breach because my ego still gets the upper hand sometimes. (For me, "ego" could well stand for "Edge God Out.") I am also trying to change my behavior to match my heart for Jesus. I'm not about to earn a halo any time soon, but even my wife, Cindy, says she detects improvement.

With the benefit of hindsight, I realize that there are many different ways to develop a heart for Jesus. Prayer, meditation, attendance at Mass, the Eucharist, any number of individual ministries, and discipling with others both inside and outside the parish are just a few. Isn't it great that all of these activities are available at one's local parish? There's a veritable cornucopia of opportunities to grow spiritually.

It's a long road, often walked with baby steps, but the desire to know Jesus is there. I know he walks beside me.

3

—

YEARNING FOR MORE

You have to consider where people are on their spiritual journey.
You can't feed people steak when they're still eating baby food.
So you have adult faith formation programs that are feeding people baby food, and then you have [programs] where people are
eating the steak and baked potato in the twenty-four-week Bible
studies. Not everyone's going to be ready to jump into a Bible
study that is that in-depth, that has homework every single week
for an hour and a half for twenty-four weeks. But they may be willing to come for an hour, once a month, to something.
—Fr. Gary Kastl
St. Anne, Broken Arrow, Oklahoma

It's exciting to be around a person who is new to faith. Like anyone
new to a love relationship, a person awakening to faith experiences
joy and amazement. He or she wants to know more, deepen this new
experience, take it all in. As disciples of Jesus Christ, newly converted
Catholics enter into a period traditionally called *mystagogia*, a time
for deepening their commitment to a new way of living and being.

But like all of us who have experienced the ups and downs of any
kind of love relationship, longtime committed Catholics can become
complacent and distracted, putting our spiritual growth on life's back
burner. When we begin to rely on our attendance at Sunday liturgy
as our personal assurance that we are right with God, we lose sight of
our deeper spiritual yearnings.

SOMETHING'S HAPPENING HERE

One of the more inspirational findings of our study was that a full 90.4 percent of our pastors consider the spiritual growth of their people to be the strongest characteristic of their communities. Pastors spoke fondly of long-term parishioners being reawakened to the desire and thirst for a deeper relationship with Christ and a greater understanding of what it means to be a disciple.

The word *disciple* comes from the Greek, meaning "learner, pupil, student." A disciple is one who has a heart for Christ and is intentionally focused on her or his own spiritual formation.[1] A recent publication by the Barna Group cited the following as the top-ranked description of discipleship among non-Catholic Christians: "Discipleship is a lifelong process and journey rooted in a relationship with Jesus."[2] For our purposes, we use the terms *spiritual growth* and *discipleship* somewhat interchangeably to indicate the process by which individuals or parishes deepen their faith, become closer to Jesus, and draw others to him as they mature in their faith.

Fr. John Riccardo of Our Lady of Good Counsel in Plymouth, Michigan, commented: "I think there's a great hunger and a great docility. For a place that's this affluent and this educated—and this is a really highly educated area—to be this teachable is pretty remarkable to me." The yearning for spiritual growth that Fr. Riccardo has tapped into is deep. He continued: "The common thing I [keep] hearing over and over again is, 'Father, we don't know; we just want to be taught.' I go, 'Wow. That's not what I was anticipating.' Something's happening here, and we're aware of it, and we want more."

While 90.4 percent of the pastors in our database believe their parishes have a strong and successful emphasis on helping people grow closer to Christ and mature in their faith, three out of four (76.6 percent) told us that there is a need for continued growth in this area. These pastors understand that discipleship is not a goal to achieve but a dynamic journey in faith. No matter where people are on their individual faith journeys, there is always room to go deeper. This chapter presents our respondents' wisdom about what parish leadership and parishioners can do to deepen discipleship.

Viewed together, these two percentages indicate that discipleship is the central focus of vibrant parishes—an area in which they simultaneously excel *and* see potential for more growth toward spiritually mature faith. All parishes likely have at least two sets of people in their pews. First, there are the people who have not as yet shown any outward interest in the spiritual growth opportunities offered by the parish. This group needs relevant, entry-level spiritual development opportunities. Second, there are those who have indeed shown interest and have become involved. Perhaps they are in small faith-sharing groups, do mission work, or are engaged in outreach. This group of parishioners continues to need ongoing spiritual development opportunities, which may look different from the opportunities designed for those newly engaged in the parish.

PLANNING FOR DISCIPLESHIP

From our interviews with pastors we learned that strategic planning is essential for deepening discipleship. How do parishes accomplish this strategic planning? They have parish leaders who do the following:

- acknowledge spiritual maturity as a goal to be pursued

- allocate resources (human and financial) to support spiritual growth initiatives

- implement strategies and campaigns that respond to the current needs of their parishioners

- repeat with new strategies and campaigns

SET SPIRITUAL MATURITY AS A GOAL

Before a goal can be pursued, it must be defined and acknowledged as something important to strive for. To pursue spiritual growth toward maturity for the parish, parish leaders must declare it a goal. Forty-four of our pastors (18 percent) used the metaphor of hunger to describe the need they saw in their parishioners for ongoing spiritual growth.

Pastors see their leadership of the community as tied intimately to the spiritual hunger of their parishioners. Fr. Michael Woods of All Saints parish in Knoxville, Tennessee, spoke as follows about making spiritual growth a goal: "I'm seeing a rise in adult participation in the faith, a desire and a hunger to learn it and live it. That's what I see happening, and I see it happening in our parish. I think it is the movement of God's spirit within our parish. . . . I think I brought a spirituality to our parish—that's what people tell me. If leadership creates its own culture, I think that I have somehow done it. People followed me into that hunger for Jesus and outreach from Jesus to each other. Jesus is the center of it." Fr. Woods's ability to lead by example in this area drew his parish down the discipleship path, deepening the spiritual culture of the parish as a whole.

Many pastors we spoke with recognize that the goal of spiritual growth is tied in to grander parish plans. "I really want to focus on spiritual renewal, with some sort of parish mission about a year from now as a focal point," said Fr. Daniel Andrews of Sacred Heart parish in Norfolk, Nebraska. "A weeklong mission, which would lead to a sense of recommitment for those who are currently active and reach out to those who are not." Fr. Andrews hoped to ignite a spiritual renewal in those whose faith has stagnated.

Some pastors we spoke with have shifted their efforts from a programmatic learning style to an emphasis on individual spiritual growth. Fr. Thomas Santen of St. Joseph parish in Manchester, Missouri, talked about how Pope Francis has helped him identify this change of attitude: "[Our goal is] getting people to become intentional members of the parish, committed to their own spiritual growth and to being part of the vision of what the parish is about, and what Church is about, in our world. I think our Holy Father is providing some great leadership, great writing stuff. I just finished [*Evangelii Gaudium*], and also his interview in *America*, and that's going to be the area that we need to really put our energy into."

Parishes often provide community building and educational opportunities, assuming that involvement in these activities will naturally deepen a sense of discipleship in participants. Many of the pastors interviewed turned this assumption upside down. They begin by directing financial and human resources into spiritual growth initiatives. They start by addressing the spiritual hunger in their parishioners. As a faith grows and a deepened understanding of discipleship develops, many parishioners become more committed to the life and mission of the parish community.

Given the busyness of parish life, it can often be the case that parish leaders, catechists, and parishioners rely on long-running programs that repeat yearly without change. The reasoning is that new people are experiencing the program each year. The pastors of our study are more likely to monitor the viability of current programs, replace those that lose importance, and keep an eye out for what new opportunities are on the horizon.

Once a parish makes the strategic decision to focus their ministries on growing the people of the parish as disciples—as Christ followers—the spiritual growth of the parish as a whole is enhanced. The terms *programming* and *activities* take on new meanings.

Although the idea of reimagining the programs and activities of a parish as ways to help people grow closer to Jesus Christ may seem like a small course correction in the life of a parish, it has potential for significant impact. This trend in the pastors we interviewed is consistent with a stunning finding that Cally Parkinson reported in *Rise: Bold Strategies to Transform Your Church*. "Increased participation in church activities *does not* significantly contribute to an increasing love of God and others," Parkinson writes. In other words, involvement in a parish program does not guarantee a parishioner's deepened commitment to Christ. Parkinson continues: "This hallmark discovery challenged and eventually changed the mind-set of thousands of church leaders."[3]

ALLOCATE RESOURCES

Once parish leadership buys into the notion of a parish-wide emphasis on disciple making and spiritual growth as well as the flexibility to continuously tweak and change, a pastor cannot simply declare, "We want growth," and expect it to happen. A key element to launching a disciple-making campaign is staff support. Fr. William Thaden of Sacred Heart Chapel in Lorain, Ohio, detailed his parish's successful four-pronged approach. First, the core team evaluates where the parish needs to grow in terms of engaging people in their relationship with the Lord. Fr. Thaden gave his core team high praise: "They're fired up. I mean, they're on fire! I've never experienced this before." Second, this parish works the process of AWE (Awaken—Witness—Evangelize), which is an ongoing strategy in which a team gives input, implements a plan, and then evaluates it. Often the outcome of AWE is to separate parishioners into small communities so that they may continue growth and be accountable. Third, the parish hires a staff member for whole-parish faith formation who surveys people about their areas of interest, reworks the kids' scripture-based curriculum, and refreshes monthly faith formation offerings for adults. Finally, the parish offers a retreat called *Living Christ* that is available four times a year in English and four times a year in Spanish. These strategies are all geared toward initiating and then continuing to nurture spiritual growth in the community.

IMPLEMENT STRATEGIES AND REVISE AS NEEDED

The goal of nurturing parishioner faith formation is not a set-it-and-forget-it kind of goal. Once articulated, the goal of encouraging discipleship must be continually revisited. Fr. Tracy O'Sullivan of St. Raphael parish in Los Angeles, California, mapped out how that works at his parish. "We take everybody where they're at," he said. "And we welcome them and accept them where they're at, always inviting them into the center to take the next step, and taking them wherever they're at and encouraging them to move ahead and take responsibility. So our parish is organized around that acceptance and power of evangelization and popular religiosity, and the customs and culture of the people, and then moving toward the Eucharist as the source and summit of the parish."

With the entire organization of the parish built around inviting individuals to take the next step to develop their relationship with

Jesus Christ, the leadership responds to parishioners' spiritual growth needs accordingly. Fr. O'Sullivan explained: "The programs and activities, missions and training—training for catechism, preparing for First Communion—are all centered around that pattern of evangelization and an encounter with Christ, through the Bible and through the Eucharist. Bible classes and other programs always are Christ-centered."

The initial step in disciple making is the decision to align all programming and training in such a way that every parish opportunity begins and ends with encountering Christ. This requires a certain amount of patience and flexibility. At one parish in the Midwest, leadership tries to anticipate next-step needs of parishioners who are actively engaged in parish life. The pastor gave the example that the working mothers in his parish needed to occasionally step outside the larger group ministries to meet more intimately as a group of women facing similar challenges.

Fr. Dan Schlegel of Holy Angels parish in Chagrin Falls, Ohio, described the need for flexibility this way: "I think that we try, to the best of our ability, to figure out how best to serve. We have an interesting quilting ministry: women get together and do quilts for the homebound, and we clothe them with that from the parish, to help them know that they're not alone, that they're clothed in the love and the prayerful support of people. There are just a zillion different things going on that really help people minister to people where they're at."

We heard from pastors who implemented multiple specific initiatives aimed at spiritual growth. One urban parish has two missions a year where speakers enrich the spirituality of their people. They also have an Adoration chapel where for the last twelve years there has been twenty-four-hour Adoration, six days per week. Another initiative at that parish is the CRHP program they do twice per year for men and for women (four in total).[4]

Consistent with the findings in *Rise*, our findings indicate a need for strategic planning for discipleship, such as building scripture-based programs and small groups. We also found a need for frank assessment and tracking of spiritual engagement in parish life through the use of a tool such as the ME[25] offered by the Gallup Corporation, described in chapter 4.

USE WHAT'S OUT THERE

The good news is that more than one hundred of our pastors (41.0 percent) found great value in programs that already exist and are available to every parish. Pastors described taking advantage of a range of strategies and programs to nurture discipleship. Multiple pastors favorably mentioned the following programs.

ACTS

Msgr. Larry Droll of St. Anne parish in Midland, Texas, spoke about the effect ACTS, a retreat program, has on his congregation: "They came from Cursillo,[5] so it starts on a Thursday night and goes until a Sunday noon, and the program is based mostly on testimonies about Adoration, community, theology, service—ACTS. And lots of spirited singing and praying and so forth. And then the genius of the ACTS retreat is that the people come back precisely to the parish, and it's in the parish where they're encouraged to get involved and follow up—to continue their spirituality."

ALPHA

Alpha is an opportunity to explore life and the Christian faith in a friendly, open, and informal environment. It runs in churches, bars, coffee shops, and homes all around the globe. Typically, Alpha has around ten sessions and includes food, a short talk, and a discussion at the end where you can share your thoughts. Alpha is for anyone who's curious. The talks are designed to encourage debate and to explore the basics of the Christian faith in a friendly, honest, and informal environment.[6]

AMAZING PARISH

Amazing Parish offers conferences for pastors and pastoral teams. These conferences feature national keynote speakers, prayer experiences, and the opportunity to meet other committed parish leaders from around the country. Each conference presents important and challenging ideas and guides a parish leadership team in the creation of the plan that they can take back to their parish.

CATHERINE OF SIENA INSTITUTE

CSI is an affiliated ministry of the Western Dominican Province dedicated to equipping parishes for the evangelization and formation of lay Catholics. The *Called & Gifted* process is designed to help Christians discern their charisms. The *Making Disciples* program is a four-day workshop that trains parish leaders to foster the awakening in others of personal faith in Christ and intentional discipleship.

CATHOLIC LEADERSHIP INSTITUTE

CLI offers leadership training to priests, deacons, and parish and diocesan leaders. Using Jesus Christ the Good Shepherd as the ultimate model of leadership, *Good Leaders, Good Shepherds* supports the ministry of Catholic priests. The *Tending the Talents* program is designed specifically for parish and diocesan leaders who work with priest graduates of *Good Leaders, Good Shepherds*. The curriculum complements the primary leadership skills and practices that priests learn in *Good Leaders, Good Shepherds*, thereby enabling all leaders of the parish or diocese to share a common leadership culture. CLI is in the process of developing a Disciple Maker Index, which will give parishes a snapshot of whether parishioners feel that they are growing spiritually. The survey will also provide information to the pastor on which aspects of parish life are growing and which are not. Parishes will be encouraged to repeat the survey every few years to chart their progress.

CATHOLICISM: ADULT STUDY PROGRAM

Bishop Robert Barron created an adult study program out of his video series *Catholicism*, which provides a thematic presentation of what Catholics believe and why so all adults can come to a deeper understanding of the Catholic faith. Not a video lecture, Church history discussion, or scripture study, this engaging and interesting formational program uses the art, architecture, literature, music, and all the treasures of the Catholic tradition to illuminate the timeless teachings of the Church.[7]

CHRIST RENEWS HIS PARISH

Pastors of vibrant parishes throughout the Midwest—from Ohio to Indiana to Wisconsin—mentioned the CRHP retreat. CRHP is a parish renewal process that features separate retreats for men and women geared toward deepening discipleship. The retreats provide an entry experience into what the Catholic Church teaches and a faith formation process where participants are encouraged to discern involvement in future ministries.

CHRISTLIFE

ChristLife offers Discovering Christ, a seven-week experience that invites guests to hear the Good News and personally encounter Jesus Christ. Discovering Christ is for anyone, from the baptized in the pews to the unbaptized person who has never entered the Church. Discovering Christ helps participants enter into or renew a personal relationship with Jesus Christ. It also gives participants the relational support necessary to begin living for Christ within the parish or group that offers the course.[8]

CORNERSTONE RETREATS

In the West many of our parishes have had success with Cornerstone retreats, which are held separately for men and women. It is a twenty-six-hour retreat that provides members of a parish with the opportunity to reflect, renew, and strengthen their faith while meeting other members of the community. Retreatants share stories and experiences of trying to live the Gospel amid the challenges of the modern world. There are a number of opportunities over the weekend to examine one's relationship with God, with family, and with others in life.

DIVINE RENOVATION

This engaging book, written by Fr. James Mallon, is a guide for parishes that are looking to cultivate communities of discipleship and vibrant, dynamic faith. Fr. Mallon challenges us to rethink our models of parish life. He is developing an international conference for parishes that share a passion for the New Evangelization and want to renew themselves. There is much more coming from Fr. Mallon and St. Benedict Church, Halifax, Nova Scotia, in the future.

DYNAMIC CATHOLIC

Popular Catholic speaker and writer Matthew Kelly has developed a series of programs and resources designed to reengage disengaged Catholics and transform marginally engaged Catholics into dynamic Catholics. For eight years, Dynamic Catholic has been making it possible for parishes and dioceses to distribute great Catholic books to parishioners and visitors at Easter and Christmas Mass through the Dynamic Catholic Book Program. More than ten million books have been distributed. Each year more than five thousand parishes participate in this simple, affordable process designed to transform parishes.

PARISH CATALYST

Parish Catalyst invites pastors and pastoral team members who are working in vibrant parishes to join a Parish Catalyst Learning Community. Parish teams hear elite speakers and leaders from various industries and religions and collaborate with other high-impact teams from across the country. Participants challenge each other to capitalize on new ideas and stretch their visions of ministry and parish leadership beyond the current strategies in play at their parishes.

PARISH SUCCESS GROUP

Parish Success Group founder Rich Curran built successful ministries for more than twenty years before founding Parish Success Group. He's had to learn by trial and error what works best for the tasks of budgeting, fundraising, recruitment, and marketing. Parish Success Group distills those real-world lessons into practical skills and solutions delivered in hands-on training for building great teams and great ministries.[9]

THE REBUILT MOVEMENT

Drawing on the wisdom gleaned from thriving megachurches and innovative business leaders while remaining rooted in the Catholic faith, Fr. Michael White and lay associate Tom Corcoran wrote *Rebuilt* in 2013. This groundbreaking book tells the inspiring story of how they brought their parish back to life. In response to the massive appeal of their first three books and the enthusiasm of the hundreds of parishes they have worked with since, White and Corcoran, along with other leaders at Church of the Nativity in Timonium, Maryland, have started the Rebuilt Parish Association. This young but growing association is designed to equip pastors and lay leaders of Catholic parishes worldwide with resources, mentoring, community forums, and guidance.

RELIGIOUS ED REWORKED

Some pastors and their catechetical teams succeeded in spurring renewed spiritual growth though reimagining and overhauling traditional religious education (RE) programs. Fr. Bob Stagg of Church of the Presentation in Upper Saddle River, New Jersey, spoke proudly about his parish's creative RE program aimed at youth. Inaugurating a "family faith formation" program, the parish abandoned the traditional model where children are dropped off once a week for religion classes and sacramental preparation. The new model brings parents and children onto campus once a month, offering various creative opportunities and activities over four nights. During the rest of the month, parents and children make use of the church's website. The website offers specific RE tools with scripture, validation games (such as a "Where does this go in the church?" game), and quizzes that children, who are all digital natives, prefer to textbooks and older methods of RE. Additionally, RE at this parish is incorporated into other initiatives in the parish community. The parish recently became a Green Faith sanctuary after a two-year certification process that involved installing a passive solar water-heating system, environmental-justice programming, worship experiences, and recycling. They tie these environmental programs (such as a night called "About Water") into RE to nurture young people in their spiritual growth as well as give them the opportunity to interact with the wider parish community.

Many adults at our parishes gravitate to adult RE programs for spiritual nourishment. Fr. Paul Manning of St. Paul Inside the Walls in Madison, New Jersey, empowered a few professionals to extend their expertise to fellow parishioners by creating their own RE program for adults: "Our Outreach to Catholic Lawyers, run by lawyers themselves, has done two remarkable programs in the last two years: a fictional 'Trial of God' that tried to prove or disprove his existence, conducted by notable local attorneys and judges, and an imagined 'Trial of the Apostle Peter,' envisioning his prosecution by the Roman Empire for a capital crime." Both of those mock trials drew hundreds of parishioners, as spectators and participants, all genuinely enjoying these spiritual growth opportunities.

THE POWER OF BELONGING

Pastors who are pleased with the spiritual growth they see in their congregations describe tight-knit communities that are involved, caring, and prayerful. Fr. Donald Snyder of St. Ladislas parish in Westlake, Ohio, notices when his parishioners are involved: "I think their strength is their frequent commitment to be engaged spiritually. We have a Generations of Faith program;[10] we had good participation. We just finished the *Catholicism* series with great participation in that program. So they come to missions. They seem to have a commitment to their own spiritual growth."

This parish is not unique. Many pastors we spoke with had parishioners who did not need convincing: they were eager and willing to take part in the spiritual opportunities offered to them. We found that parishioners can take greater responsibility for their own faith formation by actively engaging in the spiritual growth opportunities available at their parishes, specifically through the following:

- involvement in programming that nurtures discipleship
- engagement in a prayerful parish culture

- participation in community building

In other words, parishioners can grow spiritually through involvement in the scripture-based faith formation initiatives described in the previous sections, joining the retreats, attending the religious education classes, and signing up to pray at Adoration. Many parishes are also capitalizing on the benefits of small groups and missions as tools for spiritual growth. Getting involved in disciple-making offerings implemented by the parish can be the starting point for a deeper encounter with Christ.

SMALL GROUPS

Active and tight-knit small groups came up in 61.5 percent of our interviews.[11] Some parishes, such as St. Albert the Great in North Royalton, Ohio, perceive small groups as the solution to discipleship and engagement concerns. Their pastor, Fr. Ed Estok, commented, "The parish council has done some serious reflection on the challenge of engagement. I call it the science of engagement: how human beings get this sense of belonging. And the parish council has identified small groups as the principle tool [for] belonging, so that the community will become a community of communities and so that people will get the sense of belonging not to the whole big group but to their small group." This finding is widespread. Small groups act as a bridge to belonging, which leads to a deepened sense of discipleship.

One of our parishes located in New York City is surrounded by high-rise apartment buildings. When the pastor and parish team began to focus on developing small groups, one of the team members decided to invite people who live in her apartment complex—be they parishioners or not—to begin a small group in her home. She was pleased at how many people wanted to be involved. Last time we spoke with her she was encouraging other parishioners in other apartment complexes to do the same. In this case, the small groups formed out of proximity and convenience, but the groups' potential to be spiritually transformative remained as high as in other examples our research highlighted.

At Holy Family parish in Inverness, Illinois, Fr. Terence Keehan spoke to us about the depth and variety of the adult spirituality programs his parish offers. The parish has eighty small Christian communities, each with approximately fifteen people. Most groups gather every week to pray, eat, and watch a DVD accompanied by a booklet with scripture readings and questions for discussion. Fr. Keehan shared how this format has influenced parishioners' spiritual growth: "People come here and find a home in one of those small groups." This particular parish has more than 4,200 registered households and Mass attendance that routinely tops 2,500 people over an ordinary weekend. Particularly in large parishes such as this one, small groups offer a critical opportunity for spiritual development in a more intimate and personal setting. In this small-group context, the pastor explained, "they still feel like they're doing things to address their own spiritual journey or their spiritual needs." This basic protocol has enabled a large parish to break itself down into more intimate communities in which individuals can discover their own paths to deepen discipleship.

In the Northeast there is a parish where most small groups form around specific programs. For example, the parish boasts an active scripture study group, a men's group, and a Discovering Christ group. The members of these preexisting programs essentially belong to built-in small groups; however, the pastor there described his desire to develop a parish-wide initiative to offer every parishioner a chance to join a small group. The pastor said he envisions ways to eventually connect Sunday Masses back to the small groups, effectively extending the message of the homily through the week. This vision and push for inclusivity speaks to the effectiveness of small groups at encouraging the spiritual growth of participants.

Coordination of small groups is essential to their continued viability. Most of our parishes with successful small-group ministries have a dedicated staff member who coordinates them. Sometimes called the adult faith formation coordinator, this person not only helps parishioners find groups but also encourages groups to get together and provides resources for them. This liaison is particularly helpful in large parishes because he or she breaks down the anonymity to allow parishioners to connect on an individual level.

Small groups allow parishioners to stitch together squares they can call their own on the larger parish quilt, but they also give their members more immediate access to others on similar journeys of spiritual growth.

MISSIONS

Missions can be spiritually inspirational and moving on a visceral level, sticking with parishioners long after the mission work is completed and informing their spiritual growth indefinitely. Discussed in sixty-eight of the interviews (27.9 percent),[12] mission work is an effective way to deepen discipleship. Experiencing ministry through helping others in a different environment can have a profound impact on the helper.

Fr. Tony Zimmer, pastor of St. Anthony on the Lake parish in Pewaukee, Wisconsin, recounted how his parish's relationship with a sister parish in Peru has spurred spiritual growth in families who have participated in a family-to-family sponsorship program. Although his parish has built a hospice, a school, and an orphanage for the sister parish, the pastor insists that it is his parishioners who have received the larger gift of spiritual growth: "We've received far more than we've ever given, and this has been an incredible relationship, but again, it's an example of the people who are so generous here and so have a desire to make this world a better place. So that's what has been the gift that I received: that sense of a benevolent community." People can experience Christ in a more intimate way when they find themselves acting on the fundamental Christian message to make the world a better place.

Those seeking this kind of spiritual awakening do not need to fly out of the country. Fr. Ron Lewinski of St. Mary of the Annunciation parish in Mundelein, Illinois, remembers how "charged up and ready to go" forty-two kids from his parish were when they went on a mission a couple states away. Fr. Lewinski then searched for ways to get adults at his parish charged up in a similar fashion through mission work.

We will delve further into missions in part IV, but it is imperative to remember that mission work does not merely consist of an outward show of spiritual goodwill; it also carries an inward momentum for personal growth. Missions are effective places to encounter Christ.

DEEPENING AND EXPANDING COMMUNITY

In vibrant parishes, the people themselves and the culture they build create an environment where faith has the freedom and opportunity to grow. In other words, parishioners advance their own spiritual journeys and support the formation of those around them by contributing to the parish's prayerful culture.

Nearly three out of every four pastors interviewed (73.2 percent) talked about the strong sense of community that existed in their parishes. The takeaway here is that the whole is greater than the sum of its parts. A strong sense of community is associated with parish identification, bonds of friendship, interdependence, and occasions for parishioners to nurture as well as be nurtured in spiritual growth.

In a tight-knit community, opportunities for spiritual growth are not limited to what people hear on Sunday. They extend naturally into the rest of the week, as parishioners are not merely together at Mass but also friends outside of church—socializing together; participating in faith-sharing groups, Bible study groups, or service projects; sharing meals; doing neighborly favors for each other; and being there for family milestones such as births, weddings, and deaths.

The *Catechism of the Catholic Church* puts it this way: "Participation in the communal celebration of the Sunday Eucharist is a testimony of belonging and of being faithful to Christ and to his Church. The faithful give witness by this to their communion in faith and charity. Together they testify to God's holiness and their hope of salvation. They strengthen one another under the guidance of the Holy Spirit" (*CCC*, 2182).

While every individual is on his or her own spiritual journey, those who experience faith in a community—where friendships and relationships develop—have their spirituality supported in important ways. Friends go out to dinner together. Babies are christened. Birthdays are celebrated. Loved ones are mourned. Life is celebrated and growth affirmed. God is present. And Christian community thrives.

For our vibrant parishes, the faith development opportunities they offer are often community-building opportunities as well. Fr. Tony Zimmer of St. Anthony on the Lake in Pewaukee, Wisconsin, explained how his parish orients those programs and events toward community building: "We want to form community; we want to form relationships not only with each other but with God and our Lord, and so, whether it's a mission trip, whether it's a fundraising event, whether it's a golf outing, whether it's a fish fry or worship on Sunday, it's all about community and building community and building relationships." The notion here is that every parish activity is a new opportunity to bring the community closer together.

Family is the model for community building at a parish in Chicago: "Everyone understands the importance of the family; and then [we move] beyond that to understand the parish community; and . . . beyond that to understand our identity as Catholics in the local Church, as well as the global Church; and then finally [to understand] our sense of community—because we minister in a particular area— of the neighborhood." This pastor defines two communities to build: the parish community and the immediate neighborhood community. Indeed, it is important to establish the former before addressing the latter. However fragmented and needy the larger community might be, it is essential to build community within the parish first.

Well-built parish communities can withstand the test of time and geographic challenges if they are willing to change as the community around them changes. A parish we spoke with in a city in the West emphasized that the strong sense of community that exists at their parish is rooted in the 105-year-old history of the church. Both descendants of original founders and new people to the neighborhood have joined together to continue the community traditions despite the parish's location in a transient section of town. As the pastor explained, the community there is deeply dedicated to answering the question, "How do we help one another grow in being disciples of Jesus?" When a community is built around such a central, mission-driven quest, spiritual growth in the parish can thrive.

When the parish community thrives, the effect can be contagious. The pastor himself can feel moved by the parish's togetherness, as was the case with Msgr. Lloyd Torgerson of St. Monica's parish in Santa Monica, California; he had this to say: "I have an extraordinary desire to continue to serve the folks at this community. It's trying to make sure that the message of Christ, who was always talking about the mercy and the forgiveness of this loving God, is uppermost in everything that I say and do. And so it's all there. It's the Catholic ministries, people I serve, it's community, it's friendships, it's all of that. It's just a great life. It couldn't be better." Such comprehensive enthusiasm toward not only the individuals at a parish but the sense of community that exists there is a testament to how a healthy parish enriches the lives of every single person it touches, pastors included. When a community is unified in the pursuit of spiritual growth, a prayerful culture can take root.

THE POWER OF PRAYER

A CULTURE OF PRAYER

Once a community is established with a deep desire to experience God, prayer becomes even more critical. In a prayerful parish, it is apparent even to new people visiting that something special is taking place. Msgr. Stephen Knox of St. Mary parish in Huntley, Illinois, explained how a prayerful culture manifests itself at his parish: "It's a real active parish, so there's a lot of participation, a lot of good ministry stuff going on, and involvement. I'd say it's a pretty prayerful community. I think that's what new people sense. There's a nice spirit in the air, and I think that comes from our people's relationship with the Lord overflowing into the atmosphere a little bit." The overflow this pastor describes appeals to parishioners, new and existing, who seek spiritual growth.

The spirit of a deepened prayer culture comes over a Christian community at various times and for various reasons. Sometimes, as in the formation of communities themselves, it emerges when individuals, families, or groups of friends find themselves more committed to prayer. They find themselves more engaged in the Sunday experience, arriving early and staying late to participate in conversations after Mass. Confession, Adoration, Bible study, or contemplative prayer becomes, sometimes for the first time, important to them.

A core group of people who exhibit strength in prayer and follow-through can go a long way in establishing a prayerful tone at a parish. A pastor in the Northeast whom we spoke with explained that the seventy-five to 120 people who attend daily Mass drive the culture at his parish. This core group of people is fervent enough in their prayer that it has influenced the whole of his parish.

Although the Eucharist is the central experience of any Catholic parish, in a parish where prayer has a renewed significance, the Eucharist comes even closer to being the "source and summit" of the Christian life of the people. It motivates and undergirds everything, including community service and mission work. The Eucharist is the source of unity for the parish; it is the supreme action that unites all who experience it to Christ and to the prayer and tradition of the universal Catholic community.

THE PRIVILEGED PLACE OF EUCHARISTIC ADORATION

Offering Eucharistic Adoration, including perpetual Adoration (twenty-four hours per day, every day of the week) at some parishes, has proven to effectively nurture parishioners' spiritual development. Nearly one-third of the pastors we interviewed (32 percent) brought up the topic of Adoration at their parish. There may be more parishes in the sample that offer Adoration—we did not ask, "Do you have Adoration?" as part of our protocol.[13]

Eucharistic Adoration had its beginnings in the early Church. The Franciscan archives credit St. Francis of Assisi with starting Eucharistic Adoration in the thirteenth century in Italy. Despite all the changes in the modern Church, this ancient tradition continues to resonate with people in parishes we studied.

One pastor we spoke with credits Adoration with improving the overall Mass attendance at his parish in the suburban Midwest. Every week, approximately five hundred different people sign up to pray before the Blessed Sacrament. He mentioned noticing markers of spiritual growth in his parishioners: people who he guesses have not prayed much in a long time sitting and reading the Bible, as well as others in serious, prolonged prayer. Perhaps it is the opportunity for peace in a world otherwise full of noise and distractions; perhaps it is a way outside of Mass for Catholics to experience the Real Presence of Christ in the Eucharist; but whatever the reason, Adoration nurtures the spiritual lives of many.

Fr. Tom Lilly at St. Elizabeth Ann Seton in Anchorage, Alaska, said that his church began perpetual Adoration nine years earlier, and it had a profound effect on Fr. Lilly's own spiritual growth: "It's not just you adoring the Lord; the Lord adores you as his beloved son or daughter. So I think that notion of you reaching out or praising God and letting God reach out and touch and adore you—I think that intimacy and that love is what keeps me balanced and energized and motivated and on track. Centering the parish around the Eucharist means centering the parish around Christ, where a community can form around him to worship and adore him." Fr. Lilly's enthusiasm for Adoration likely impacts his parishioners' appreciation and understanding of perpetual Adoration.

Along the same lines, Fr. Paul Duchschere of Sts. Anne and Joachim parish in Fargo, North Dakota, considers Adoration the foundation on which the entire health of his parish rests:

> The founding pastor started Adoration right away, even before they had a place to have a church. He made it work, and it's been going for fifteen years. It's wonderful, and it kind of runs itself. We get new people on a regular basis. And that's the reason this parish is so healthy. This is the healthiest parish I've ever been to. Are there problems? Of course there are problems. But it's the healthiest, happiest parish I've ever been to, and

I have absolutely no doubt it's because of the foundation of the two-hundred-some people that adore the
Lord in the Eucharist Monday through Friday.

It seemed that Fr. Duchschere could not overstate the importance
of Adoration in deepening the discipleship of his parishioners. He
had a message for those pastors hesitant about bringing Adoration to
their parishes: "You don't need it, per se. But boy, without it, you're
missing something. If you've got people willing to come and spend
time with Jesus, things are going to happen."

CRUCIAL TAKEAWAYS

1. 90 percent of our pastors identified the spiritual growth of their
    parishioners as the number-one strength of their parishes.

2. Engaging the spiritual hunger of parishioners increases their par-
    ticipation in parish community life and outreach. But the converse
    is not true: involvement in parish activities does not necessarily
    equate to growth in a person's spiritual development.

3. The spiritual growth of a faith community is a flexible, ongoing
    dynamic that needs to be continually reevaluated, updated, and
    altered in order to satisfy the spiritual hunger of the people.

4. When parishes earmark funds and staffing for spiritual develop-
    ment, the growth that follows impacts all other aspects of parish life.

5. More than a hundred of our pastors (41 percent) have used exist-
    ing renewal programs, processes, or consulting services to nur-
    ture spiritual growth and commitment.

6. Discipleship flourishes where people experience a deep sense of
    belonging.

7. A parish culture rooted in fervent prayer, particularly Eucharis-
    tic Adoration, creates tight-knit communities focused on spiritual
    maturing and discipleship.

4

CHALLENGES TO ENGAGEMENT, SPIRITUAL MATURITY, AND DISCIPLESHIP

One of the greatest opportunities overall is engagement, and one of the significant challenges is the opposite of that, which would be apathy. [There are] people who don't want to get involved, they don't have the time to get involved, or they don't feel the need to get involved. Overall it's engagement—getting people engaged in the life of the parish and in their own faith.
—Fr. Mark Reamer, O.F.M.
St. Francis of Assisi, Raleigh, North Carolina

For many years, one of our pastors lived a lukewarm priesthood, a cultural priesthood. Even though he accomplished many things, he had not given his heart completely to Christ. He woke up fifteen minutes before he would preside at eight o'clock Mass, not knowing what he would preach on. Not having read the scriptures beforehand, he would glance over a commentary and preach whatever it suggested. He served "leftovers" weekdays and Sundays alike.

Then, about a decade ago, he met with a spiritual director who told him after a quick meeting, "You know, you and I are done with our work." Confused, the pastor asked him to clarify. The spiritual director looked him in the eye and told him, "When you speak of God,

I don't feel it. When you speak of Christ, I don't feel Christ in your heart. I don't see Christ in your eyes." The pastor was outraged and stormed out. For the next six months he did not speak to the spiritual director.

Not long after this encounter, the pastor had a heart attack. Then he had another. Although he survived, he recovered slowly at a priest retirement center, where one of the other resident priests began to support him. Laying his hands on the recovering pastor, he asked, "What do you want?" The pastor told him he wanted a new heart.

Of course, the pastor meant he wanted a new physical heart, but the truth was twofold: his spiritual heart was also broken. When he physically recovered, his relationship with Christ was still in limbo, so he decided to attend an eight-day retreat. Laying it all before the Lord, he heard Jesus say to him, "I can make you well. I can restore your priestly identity."

He began to mend spiritually. It was gradual, but the more he risked stepping out into faith, the stronger his faith became. Recently a woman challenged him: "You know, you talk about the New Evangelization. Is that all words or do you really believe it?"

His reply was as clear as it was profound: "It saved me."

SLEEPWALKING THROUGH FAITH

The spiritual apathy expressed in this pastor's story appears to reside in many of the well-intentioned, Mass-attending Catholics sitting in the pews of our churches today. Though disciplined about Mass attendance, many do not appear to be moving forward on a dynamic journey of faith.

Alongside the concern that pastors have for those who have left the Church altogether, pastors struggle with how to combat the spiritual stagnation they see in many of the people who remain faithful Mass attenders. They expressed worry that people are merely checking a box or fulfilling requirements without much energy or passion. Pastors described some of their Mass-attending parishioners as "punching their time card," their only aim being to "fulfill my duty." One Texas pastor described Mass attendees as "sleepwalking" through their faith: "We want to make sure that people understand that it is not just about showing up for Mass on a Sunday or throwing a few bucks in the collection plate or anything. There's more to life in a Catholic parish than that, and so that's what we're working hard on: [getting] people more engaged, more involved."

When apathy afflicts a congregation, it is a sign that spiritual needs are not being met. According to a Pew study, among former Catholics who are now Protestant, 71 percent say they left Catholicism because their spiritual needs were not being met, making this the group's most commonly cited reason for leaving the Catholic Church.[1] The greatest concern with the passive Mass attender is that he or she will switch from weekly to monthly to seasonal church attendance and at that point leave the Church altogether.

An individual's spiritual growth is as difficult to measure as it is to define. Pastors have long been concerned with the spiritual growth of their flock; what is new is the attempt to quantify this growth. The idea of creating a survey that can measure spiritual development and then provide parishes with a branded product or kit to track and increase an individual's or a community's spiritual growth is a recent one. The seeds were sown in the 1980s and 1990s, but the practice did not fully take off until the 2000s, with tactics developed by senior ministers at Willow Creek Community Church in South Barrington, Illinois, in their groundbreaking book *Move*.

Since then, measuring spiritual growth and engagement in parish life has become a hot topic in the Catholic Church. In recent years many groups—Catholic, nondenominational Christian, and corporate—have developed measurement tools. Each measurement tool has its own set of definitions and standards. Four of the most popular tools are represented in table 4.1.

The findings in table 4.1 point unanimously to low levels of spiritual engagement. On the low end of these figures, we find that 0.04 percent of church-attending US Catholics are considered "disciple makers" by CLI, and 7 percent are "dynamic Catholics" according to Matthew Kelly. Gallup's Member Engagement Survey, also known as

Table 4.1 Measuring spiritual growth and engagement in parish life

	Author or organization			
	Matthew Kelly	Willow Creek	Gallup	Catholic Leadership Institute
Text or survey	*The Four Signs of a Dynamic Catholic**	REVEAL[†]	ME[25‡]	Disciple Maker Index[§]
Definition of spiritual growth or engagement	The individual's routine includes daily prayer, Bible study, generosity, and evangelization.	The individual has achieved the highest level on the spiritual continuum— Christ-centered: "My relationship with Jesus is the most important relationship in my life. It guides everything I do."	"Engaged members" are loyal and have a strong psychological connection to their parish. They are more spiritually committed, more likely to invite friends, family members, and coworkers to parish events, and give more both financially and in commitment of time.	"Disciple makers" are people who are formed to form others as disciples of Jesus.
Average score	7% of all Catholics are "dynamic Catholics"	25% of congregants in Willow Creek's REVEAL database are "Christ-centered"	18% of all Catholics are "engaged members"**	0.04% of all US Catholics are "disciple makers"

* Matthew Kelly, *The Four Signs of a Dynamic Catholic* (Hebron, KY: Beacon Publishing, 2012).

† REVEAL is the name of the database where these findings are collected. The REVEAL statistics are reported in both *Move* (p. 50) and *Rise* (in press).

‡ "The ME[25] Member Engagement Survey consists of 25 questions that were carefully chosen to measure engagement as well as spiritual commitment and outcomes important to faith communities." Gallup, accessed April 29, 2016, http://www.gallup.com/products/174866/faith-member-engagement.aspx.

§ The Disciple Maker Index shows what characteristics of parishes are most strongly associated with discipleship.

** This figure is an estimate of the engagement level of *all Catholics*. Gallup gathers ME[25] data from parishes and parishioners who self-select to participate in the ME[25] survey. These parishioners are likely to be more engaged than Catholics as a whole, since they are part of a parish that is actively trying to track and increase engagement. Among these more active Catholics, the average level of parish engagement is 30%. They are more engaged than Catholics as a whole, but still this higher figure represents a sign of hope—some parishes are already there, and many more could attain that level of engagement.

ME[25], shows a more robust engagement level: 18 percent of church-going Catholics.[2]

RECOGNIZING AN UNDERVALUED ASSET

Although these numbers are distressing, they can also be viewed as an incredible opportunity for parishes to reach out to and have a profound impact on literally millions of American Catholics.

From my years in the investing world, I know to seek out the sweet spot where a small outlay can yield a large return; I have spent the last thirty years looking for opportunities to invest in assets the marketplace has undervalued. Such opportunities are safe bets in that they generally have very little downside and a lot of upside. Anytime numbers are this low, it does not take much to double or even triple them. That is how I look at spiritual growth and engagement numbers.

Regardless of the method of measurement, it is hard to imagine these percentages going lower. Let's take as an example the most optimistic statistic, from Gallup's ME[25] database, which estimates that 18 percent of all church-attending Catholics are engaged in their parishes. The undervalued asset I see here is the next 18 percent. In the investing business, we call that the chance to double. The next 18 percent are those parishioners who are a short distance away from deeper involvement. They have the desire to grow spiritually and may be willing to be more involved in their church communities. They may just need a personal invitation, simple opportunities, or a heartfelt appeal from the pulpit to encourage them to take the next step.

These parishioners are the safe bet, the Coca-Cola stock of parish renewal with whom, as Warren Buffet or his mentor Ben Graham might say, there is a meaningful margin of safety. There is very little downside and a lot of upside to developing parish initiatives that are designed to engage these members. With successful outreach to these parishioners, a parish could double its engagement from 18 percent to 36 percent (see figure 4.1).

To put it another way: were the whole of the United States a single parish, with the good, but not great, finding of 18 percent engagement, that would mean that only about twelve million (12,258,000) of the current sixty-eight million one hundred thousand parish-affiliated Catholics would be considered truly "engaged" in parish life.[3] If all the parishes in the United States looked forward and focused their pastoral efforts on the next 18 percent, twenty-four million Catholics would be revitalizing the Church.

If you had told Pastor Rick Warren of Saddleback Church in California or Pastor Bill Hybels of Willow Creek Community Church in Illinois, both of whom started their megachurches from scratch, "You're gonna start out as pastor at a church that has 1,500 people," they would have been more than excited. They would have said, "Great, the people are already there." That is the value proposition.[4] The people already there are the low-hanging fruit. It is obvious. Warren and Hybels each had to start their now-thriving congregations

Figure 4.1 Moving the engagement needle

REACH THE PRE-ENGAGED; DOUBLE CURRENT PARISH ENGAGEMENT

PRE-ENGAGED

UNENGAGED

ENGAGED

**SENSE OF BELONGING
TO A PARISH AND
COMMITMENT TO
ITS MISSION**

ONLY 18% OF ALL THOSE ATTENDING MASS ARE CONSIDERED TO BE ENGAGED IN THE PARISH.
TARGETING THE NEXT 18%, THE PRE-ENGAGED, IS AN ATTAINABLE GOAL FOR A PARISH AND IMMEDIATELY
DOUBLES THE NUMBER OF PEOPLE COMMITTED TO THE
COMMUNITY AND ITS MISSION.

from scratch. Catholic pastors, by contrast, do not have to go out and find people.

Increasing the engagement of the next 18 percent of Catholics should be the obvious first step. The trick is to stay away from the "too hard" box, to not be distracted by juggling the things that are too difficult when instead you could invest in one simple, undervalued thing that will yield large returns.

The New Evangelization is an awakening within the Church to the need to disciple our own. What we learned from pastors who are doing it well is they have taken a strategic approach to discipling their people. They are taking advantage of the opportunity to double what they have. Approximately 16 percent of the pastors mentioned the New Evangelization in their interviews. This group represents a vanguard on the cutting edge of discourse about how to encourage faith formation and help the already faithful advance their spiritual journeys.

Fr. Mark Spalding of Holy Trinity in Louisville, Kentucky, believes that when it comes to the New Evangelization, he need not look further than his own backyard. "What we have here is a significantly sized school, which has 760 kids," he said.

> We have a huge number of young parents sitting right in front of us. And what I'm always looking for is—how do I get my foot in the door, so that Christ can enter into their lives? How can I do it in a wonderful, creative way that shows that Christ is the best answer for all kinds of questions in their lives, and the kind of direction that they need, and fulfillment they can truly have. All that is found in Christ, in the Church, and so I'm just looking at our own backyard, and young parents that are here.

This pastor's observation is a good example of how the outreach called for by the New Evangelization does not have to be aimed outside the parish. School parents are perfect targets for New Evangelization efforts because of their current involvement and the potential to generate a passionate engagement.

The New Evangelization is all about creating a passion for the faith. From St. Mary's in Greenville, South Carolina, Fr. Jay Scott Newman described his parish's New Evangelization practices as a "living laboratory" where they experiment with tactics to engage parishioners until they find what works. This pastor pointed to France, where he says 90 percent of people are Catholic but only 2 percent go to Mass on Sunday, as an example of where American Catholics could head if they do not step up and find out what they can do to ingrain the New Evangelization into their parishes. He believes the way to address the many challenges the Church faces today is through changing how parishes are experienced: "The rubber meets the road at the parish. The Catholic Church is a vast abstraction until you go to the local parish. It's in the parish that it either stands or falls." In this view, all the talk of New Evangelization is meaningless if it is not enacted on a parish level.

After studying the needs of the parish for years, one pastor decided that a retreat was exactly what they needed. He spoke about his new pastoral associate, who was instrumental in coordinating new discipleship initiatives, and narrated how his parishioners moved slowly but surely to passion through this retreat. The retreat has been a huge success in growing spirituality among those who participated, and the parish goal is eventually to get every parishioner to attend.

At Queen of Peace parish in Gainesville, Florida, Fr. Jeff McGowan sees a bubbling up of passion within a specific group. In discussing the growing faith among the men at his parish, Fr. McGowan emphasized the migration from obligation to passion: "[These are] men who are more engaged in their own spiritual journey[s], and they're hungry for it. They're hungry for the camaraderie of other men, and they're hungry for the greater knowledge and personal movement toward the Lord, and I think that's a tremendous trend, and none of it is obligation. Anybody who's there for that, they're there because they want to be." The men at this parish exhibit precisely what the New Evangelization intends to accomplish.

REACHING THE FENCE-SITTERS

The Gallup Corporation gathers ME[25] data from the self-selected parishes and parishioners who have chosen to participate in the ME[25] survey. These parishioners are likely to be more engaged than the general church-attending Catholic population, since they belong to a parish that is likely more vibrant than the average since it is actively trying to track and increase engagement. Among these more active Catholics, the average level of parish engagement is 30 percent. This higher figure represents a sign of hope—if some parishes are already there, many more could attain that level of engagement. It is worth noting that a handful of the parishes we studied shared their Gallup ME[25] scores with us. The average engagement of these parishes, 33.5 percent, was substantially higher than the national average of 18 percent.

Fr. James Mallon of St. Benedict Church in Halifax, Nova Scotia, used the ME[25]. According to Fr. Mallon, "Gallup measures the human conditions that bring about changed beliefs. Changed beliefs bring about the spiritual behaviors that we all desire." Fr. Mallon saw his parish's engagement nearly double in a few years: "We just found out that we are at 41 percent engagement. We started with an engagement level of 24, three years ago or even less than that perhaps. So that's been a huge shift."

Msgr. Vincent Rush of Our Lady of Grace parish in West Babylon, New York, mentioned that his parish was 21 percent engaged and 41 percent actively disengaged but followed up with this description about what he saw occurring:

> A lot of the formalities of an older style of Catholicism,
> I think, are being set aside. Sometimes I think that I'm
> growing a new living parish inside the husk of an old-
> er one, and it's going to be that or a kind of shedding
> [of] a skin at some point, and a lot of the people who

are nominally Catholic in our neighborhood—once grandma dies and there's no more pressure on the grandkids to get the great-grandkids baptized—[are] going to fade away, and we're going to have a smaller but livelier parish. Not in the terms of which, let's say, Pope emeritus Benedict talked—about a smaller, purer Church, doctrinally—but in terms of a smaller, engaged church. . . . The people whose connection to the Church is only social or, even better, kind of ancestral, may well make other choices. The growing popularity of "spiritual engagement" measurements has generated conversation about how best to help people experience a deepening relationship with Christ. It has also provoked thought about parish-level planning that might help grow that relationship. Matthew Kelly offers four simple signs of a dynamic Catholic: prayer, Bible study, generosity, and evangelization. As Kelly says, "We need solutions that are accessible to all, that inspire people to say, 'I can do that!'"

Many pastors we spoke with share the longing for a more engaged congregation. One pastor at an urban parish said, "I want to move the parish to be engaged in their faith and know it, to be able to stand up for their Catholic faith and to live it. I want to move the parish to a sense of personal ownership for their faith so that they aren't just sitting out here like little birds with their mouths open, waiting to get fed—but so that they feel called to serve, for justice, and for who we need to be as a community of faith."

One pastor recounted the story of how his predecessor at a Midwestern parish was relatively inactive and unconcerned with growth. The incoming pastor saw this as an opportunity to refound the parish and felt a genuine sense of excitement. Not knowing where to start, he picked up the phone and began calling parishioners. These individuals were shocked that he called, and when he began asking specific questions about things related to the parish, he discovered that the parish was, on the whole, completely disengaged. Without having ever met these individuals, this pastor had sparked a new sense of engagement in the parish by making connections with his people.

KNITTING A PARISH TOGETHER

When parishes talk about welcome or hospitality, the first reaction is to work at making people feel welcome at Mass. But once people feel personally welcomed, developing a larger parish welcoming culture has less to do with cookies and coffee and more to do with preparing those in the pews to step outside their comfort zones and be a welcoming presence to others, especially those whose interests are different from or even in conflict with their own.

Parishes with an open and welcoming culture seek to reach all the people in their community, knitting themselves together into one unified parish. Parishes struggle with this for a variety of reasons. Our study found that the three most common obstacles to unity were multiple cultural and language groups in the parish, difficulties in developing a sense of connection and intimacy within a large congregation, and navigating parish mergers.

MULTIPLE CULTURES AND LANGUAGES

Multiple cultural and language groups make building a united parish community particularly challenging because there is a lack of continuity at the basic level of communication. This is a reality more and more American parishes are facing.

In an attempt to serve everyone, parishes often cater to different groups with Masses and ministries in the various languages spoken by parishioners. However, this solution often entrenches the separation between the groups. Pastors in our study who succeeded in leading bilingual parishes were often themselves bilingual or were drawing on the social capital of bilingual staff, lay leaders, and parishioners to foster more interaction between groups (e.g., having bilingual staff meetings and ministries as opposed to having different meetings in different languages).

Fr. Bob Tabbert's parish, St. John XXIII in Fort Myers, Florida, includes English and Vietnamese communities, with weekly Masses offered in both languages, as well as a smaller Latin American community, with one Mass in Spanish each month. He told us, "It is [a diverse parish]. And that's one of the challenges that I am faced with, and we're doing our best to make sure that we can really meld together all these communities. I don't want three different communities under one roof. I want us all to be one, respecting the cultures and different styles of worship. . . . At least twice a year, we'll do a Mass in three languages; it's always unique and fun, and it works."

Msgr. Richard Martini of St. Joseph parish in Carpinteria, California, who shepherds a community with two languages, added, "The fact that we do it in two languages automatically sets up two communities, and so there's a trick in bridging that. The people that are bilingual and can come to the English Mass, even though they speak primarily Spanish, work as a bridge. It's not enough, but [the church is] a gathering spot for people."

Cultural differences make for confusing situations when multiple cultures are combined. Tricia Wittman-Todd, pastoral life coordinator for St. Mary's Church in Seattle, Washington, described a comical situation in her parish:

> You have a lot of different cultural norms about what are accepted behaviors and what behaviors mean. So, for instance, the usual thing in the English community is that if I'm sitting at the end of the pew, unless I have a specific reason why I need to sit at the end of the pew, and someone comes, I move over, and they sit down. That would be considered polite behavior. In the Spanish community, it is not polite to do that. It is polite that you sort of move a little bit so the person can get around you. So imagine those two communities coming together. The English speaker thinks, "Why is this person crawling on me?" The Spanish community thinks, "Why are they moving? I'm trying

to get over you and now you're moving! What is this?"
So those [are] things that you don't realize until you're
in an environment where you just have very different
assumptions. So that's going to be the challenge going
forward: How do we continue to integrate?

Nonetheless, consolidating ministries and putting an end to the
silo-like structures of some parishes is a way forward for many pastors. Msgr. Henry Petter of St. Ann Church in Coppell, Texas, commented, "The other big challenge we have in this parish is trying to
make it the one parish, even though we have two languages that we're
dealing with, and lots of different cultures. So it's a challenge in every
parish that has more than one language—trying to get all of the people on one page, going in the same direction." To accomplish this, he
focused on hiring "really good people who are bilingual and bicultur-
al" and reported, "We're just now getting them on board. They have
to be bilingual, so that was the hardest thing to find, bilingual people.
We want to get away from having Hispanic ministry in our parish
that is separate from other departments. We're trying to have all our
departments be bilingual."

There was some consensus among our pastors that integrating
different language ministries allowed a parish to take a step toward
uniting the whole community and creating a sense of shared ownership. But some pastors also reported concerns with this style of community building. Fr. John Antony of Immaculate Conception Church
in Fort Smith, Arkansas, saw combining two ministries of different
languages (e.g., Spanish and English) as risky, given that people's
faith hangs in the balance. He explained:

I asked the staff when I first arrived here . . . "What
do you think we need to really work on as a parish?"
And one of the things that people kept mentioning was
bringing our two communities together, the Hispanic and the Anglo communities. But I'm not sure that's
the best way forward. I know it certainly sounds good,

and certainly I don't want to drive people apart . . . [but] the practicality of it is a mess.

Okay—bring people together. So, what language are you going to speak in? And normally, the Anglos are going to say, "Well, in English, of course. You're here in the United States." And the Hispanics are going to say, "Well, we don't speak English. We'd like to, but we don't." Well, it's a little simplistic to me to say, "Let's just bring everybody together." . . . Another reason why I'm not convinced that's the best way forward is that we didn't do this in the past. When the new culture came to the United States, we didn't force them to join an existing parish. We started a new parish for them. That's why, in most large cities, there is an Irish church and a Polish church and an Italian church. Why is that? Because the people needed to be able to express their faith through their culture. And here we're telling all our Hispanics, "Well, you just don't worry about being Hispanic, you just come and join us over here in the Anglo Church." I'm not sure that's the best thing to do because sometimes if you force someone to choose between their faith [and] their culture, they might not make the right choice.

OUTGROWING INTIMACY

Many pastors pointed to parish size as a challenge to knitting a parish together. As the old expression goes, "the larger you get, the smaller you need to be." Intimacy has been a staple of Christian communities from its earliest days; it must be fostered more deliberately and nurtured more carefully when thousands sit in the pews on Sunday.

Fr. John Riccardo of Our Lady of Good Counsel in Plymouth, Michigan, remarked:

We're too big. That's why, when you ask, "Are we growing?" I hope not. We can't grow. How do three men take care of eight thousand people? The challenge for a parish is, you do something well—which should be what every place does, so it's not extraordinary; it's just we're trying to do what we're supposed to do—you do it, and it gets a reputation, and then it grows, and then it grows, and it loses that familial sense, and then you lose the ability to really just be in there with people, because there [are] too many people. . . . That's one of the challenges of being a big church, I think.

Another pastor described his function in a large parish as one of "wearing [myself] out trying to be loving and to communicate that love and communion in more and more effective ways. [We have] a huge number of people. Communicating with them and giving them the sense of belonging is a challenge."

Fr. Richard Sullivan's parish, St. Michael in Louisville, Kentucky, sought to grow but "still maintain that sense of intimacy, closeness, and family atmosphere more typical of smaller churches." As Fr. Frederick Pausche of St. Gabriel parish in Concord Township, Ohio, remarked, "There's a fine line between a crowd and a community."

For a great number of our parishes, that sense of community has come as a byproduct of small faith-sharing groups. Fr. Steve Orr of Our Lady's Immaculate Heart Church in Ankeny, Iowa, remarked, "The small-group process has been really helpful to us because you can get lost in a place like this."

MERGERS

When parishes merge, they experience a distinct impediment to building a cohesive community. Several pastors mentioned parishioners' concerns around the dynamics of parish mergers and consolidations. Who has a voice? Who is in and who is out? When two parishes merge and use the church of one of the communities, the parishioners who have lost their own worship space often feel resentment and insecurity.

Fr. Joe Fortuna of Our Lady of the Lake parish in Euclid, Ohio, described a merger that happened rather abruptly:

> I still have a strong sense that there are people in the area who still haven't landed. Just last week, I met someone who was from the church down the street [who] said, "Since your church merged, I haven't found a place yet," and I don't think she's that unusual. The image I like to use is [that] of an arranged marriage; it's a mixture of parish cultures. I tried to be sensitive to the fact that this was to be a merge and not a swallow. We really tried to create an atmosphere where parishioners from both former parishes were treated the same way.

Perhaps predictably, this approach rankled some parishioners who felt they ought to have a bigger voice but energized some people who had previously felt voiceless but now were heard.

Fr. Steven Verhelst of St. Mary in Willmar, Minnesota, who pastors four parishes clustered in a single area, found that the challenges of merging actually kept the communities separate. He said, "As much as we want these four parishes to come together, at the same time [we are] dealing with that balance of recognizing that each of these particular parishes has a community of [its own] and a culture of [its own]. How do you honor and respect that? Ultimately . . . I think if you were to ask the people who are coming through these doors to celebrate Eucharist on Sundays, they come here because of the faces they see every Sunday and the people they pray with. That becomes Eucharist for them."

Deepening discipleship is one of the purposes of the New Evangelization. Fr. Charlie Ranges, who pastors both St. Lawrence and Holy Family parishes in Essex Junction, Vermont, called attention to the importance of remaining mindful about that: "I have this notion of Church as being the people of God. Evangelize the baptized: that's part of the mission. I think that's very much a part of me. However, we are mindful that as disciples of Jesus, God calls us to ever deeper, further growth."

CHALLENGES RECAPPED

1. Many Mass-attending Catholics, though disciplined about attending church, do not appear to be moving forward on a dynamic journey of faith.

2. Mass-attending parishioners are often undervalued as a parish asset.

3. The level of engagement in American parishes could easily be doubled by focusing on the segment of parishioners who, in their hearts, want to be engaged but have not been helped to make that next step in their spiritual journeys.

4. Even great parishes struggle to provide an open and welcoming culture. Many kinds of factions within parish communities can be difficult to knit together.

PART III

GREAT PARISHES
EXCEL ON SUNDAYS

PEACE AND QUIET

Heading out on one of our family's first trips to St. Monica's, in the midst of the usual "I don't want to go to Mass" and "I want to watch cartoons" comments, my wife, Cindy, and I managed to get everyone in the car and eventually to St. Monica's steps. The kids got out and started pushing each other. There was a lot of hitting and shoving going on—the usual chaotic, circus-like atmosphere. I said to myself, "The only reason I am doing this is because I think it's important," while my wife rolled her eyes. We eventually made it into nine-thirty Mass and sat down.

We had no idea what was going to happen. For all we knew, one of the kids was going to throw a fit and we were going to be out on the steps again. Then I heard Msgr. Torgerson say, "Would all the children please stand up?"

I looked at one of my kids and strongly whispered, "Stand up. Do what the priest says." Msgr. Torgerson continued, "You are all going with Marie Slayton over to that building because it's Sunday school." The kids left.

I looked at my wife like, "Yeah, baby. Yeah."

Our children weren't sure what the heck was going on. I didn't know what was going on either. All I knew was that the parish was taking responsibility for our kids. Perfect. My wife and I sat side by side just staring at each other. It was the first peace and quiet I remember us having in a very long time.

My wife wasn't Catholic back then, but it didn't matter: she was enjoying the Mass all the same. We felt at peace and tension-free. The parish had gifted us with an unexpected moment of quiet respite from the normal commotion of raising small children. We felt supported and connected.

Little did we know, it was just the beginning.

The friendly, generous reception we experienced that day was true hospitality. As we relate in the next chapters, parish hospitality is more than simply a spontaneous welcome. It is an intentional and strategic plan that begins long before the sun rises on a given Sunday morning.

5

A VIBRANT SUNDAY EXPERIENCE

You almost feel the energy in the church . . . that people expect
something to happen . . . a hum, you feel it in the room. And sure
enough, the liturgy begins and the Holy Spirit shows up.
                                        —Msgr. Charles Pope
                        Holy Comforter-St. Cyprian, Washington, DC

My pastor told me a great story about St. Francis of Assisi recently.
The saint was in the forest for days. He fasted. He prayed. One day,
he emerged from the forest, got on his knees, and begged God for just
a small piece of bread to give him enough energy to get back home.
Then he saw a small building with a sign hanging above the entrance:
"Fresh Bread Baked Daily Here."

Francis was beside himself with joy and praised God. He rushed
forward and knocked on the door. A woman opened. Francis told the
woman who he was and the story of how he gave away his fortune.
The woman listened patiently while he continued. He told her that
he had no money left and asked if she could spare a square of fresh
bread, only enough to fuel his return to Assisi. "I'm sorry," said the
woman, smiling, "We don't bake bread here. All we do here is make
signs that say 'Fresh Bread Baked Daily Here.'"

"No bread," she reiterated. "Just signs."

BASIC BREAD AND BUTTER

How does a parish become more than a posted sign that reads "Jesus Available Here"? How does it become an inspiring community that buzzes with life and gives off a welcoming energy that attracts people?

The first step is to take Sunday seriously.

That may sound like a truism: "Of course we take Sunday seriously." But it is easy for a parish to rely year-in and year-out on the rituals of the Mass while it slips into a tired Sunday routine. Pastors and staffs, overextended by programs, instruction, and other duties in the remaining six days of the week, have little creativity or energy left to give to the Sunday experience. The old-guard parishioners become set in their ways, comfortable in the unchanging weekly ritual of coming, receiving, and leaving.

In their bestselling book *Rebuilt*, Fr. Michael White and Tom Corcoran outline the stops and starts they took to bring their parish's Sunday experience back to life. For them it began with the courage to name the problem, "We were too busy Monday through Friday to worry about Sunday."[1] They noticed that their parishioners did not seem to be experiencing Eucharist as the "source and summit" of their religious experiences.[2]

By contrast, 76 percent of the pastors whose interviews provide the data and insights for this book mentioned the Sunday liturgy as one of their parish's greatest assets. They spoke of how important the focus on and preparation of the various aspects of each Sunday's experience is for their parish communities.

Fr. Mark Reamer, O.F.M., pastor of St. Francis of Assisi in Raleigh, North Carolina, put it succinctly: the three Hs—Hospitality, Homilies, and Hymns—are all crucial to making a Sunday worship experience extraordinary. "It's your basic bread and butter. Hospitality means that they feel welcome and want to come back. They want to get involved. Homilies give people something to chew on in terms of the preaching. And hymnody—songs people can sing and that engage them. People are coming to have the Word broken open for them [because] it has an application to their life."

This sentiment was echoed by Fr. Douglas Doussan of St. Gabriel the Archangel Church in New Orleans, Louisiana: "In our parish, people are extremely hospitable. I try to be that way and make the homilies worthwhile. Then, the music is outstanding. We have a gospel choir at the ten-thirty Mass. The music director knows music—gospel music and other genres as well—and knows liturgy. I'm telling you that's a rare combination."

ORCHESTRATING THE WELCOME

There is a lot of talk today about hospitality in the Church. We are beginning to understand that it takes a whole lot more than a friendly greeter at the door. Sixty-one percent of our pastors said they consider vibrant hospitality essential to vibrant liturgy. But developing such hospitality can require a cultural shift in the way everybody—pastor, staff, and parishioners—thinks about welcoming.

In his novel *Finnegan's Wake*, James Joyce famously wrote, "Catholic means 'Here comes everybody.'" What was true in 1930s Ireland, in the pre–Vatican Council II Church, still holds true in the twenty-first-century Church in the United States. American Catholics come in all stripes. Catholics speak so many languages that in the Archdiocese of Los Angeles alone one can find Masses in forty-two different languages and dialects.

To the mix of people, add the Church's stances on a number of social and moral issues that can evoke reactions varying from mild displeasure to outrage and defiance, and one can see how providing a welcoming environment is not always easy. Some Church stances annoy the progressively minded while some annoy the traditionally minded, but it all adds up to the reality that each person who walks through the door of a Catholic church on any given Sunday morning is a unique person, with one-of-a-kind religious and social sensibilities and expectations. Catholic may still mean "here comes everybody," but today "everybody" seems to include an even broader range of people.

Society is also becoming more individualistic, which must also affect a parish's orientation toward welcoming. People speak of *my* space, *my* time, *my* agenda, and even *my* church. Welcoming the stranger, the poor person, or the person with a radically different perspective can require a change of heart in a parish's welcoming culture.

Pope Francis said in *Evangelii Gaudium* that "if the parish proves capable of self-renewal and constant adaptivity, it continues to be 'the Church living in the midst of the homes of her sons and daughters'" (*Evangelii Gaudium*, 28).

Pastors we interviewed who exhibited strong hospitality, welcome, and overarching community spirit reported that they had an organized team of volunteers, staff, and clergy to welcome people to Sunday Mass. Many parishioners who attend vibrant parishes see a smile and a waving hand as they arrive on the parish grounds. This simple gesture does not occur spontaneously. Hospitality takes strategic organization behind the scenes. Extensive preparation and planning go into it, and much of this planning is invisible to the eyes of a visitor. A volunteer base is recruited, developed, and trained with a clear sense of the vital role of hospitality. The pastor and liturgical team encourage and train the people of the parish in creating a welcoming culture where parishioners and strangers are made to feel equally at home.

FORMING THE TEAM AND THE STRUCTURE

The pastors we spoke with are deliberate in their own efforts to model hospitality and welcome. But they also voiced the reality of how day-to-day parish work, administration, and dealing with the other pastoral care needs of their parishioners can seem all-consuming. Talented as he may be, no one pastor has the ability to answer all the parishioners' questions on arrival. "Father can handle questions," Fr. Doug LeCaptain of St. Raphael the Archangel in Oshkosh, Wisconsin, told us, "but when there are four hundred people streaming in and out of a church, I can [answer] ten or fifteen of [their questions], but that's it." The job of welcoming the entire congregation to Mass is too much for the pastor alone, but a well-organized hospitality *team* can meet this need.

Pastors mentioned simple practices that could be implemented in just about any parish. If you don't already have a ministry of greeters, create one and train them. Demonstrate warm greeting practices for other staff and volunteers, training the Eucharistic Ministers, parochial vicars, deacons, and lay leaders in the culture of welcoming. Ask all staff members to wear nametags during worship services. Come up with a welcoming slogan to convey the parish's hospitality, as one parish in Michigan has done so successfully under their pastor.

"Always loved, always welcome" communicates the warmth of the welcome at St. Anastasia in Troy, Michigan, says Fr. J. J. Mech. It permeates the parish down to the people in the pews. Fr. Mech explains that this is especially helpful for larger parishes like his, where you might come every Sunday and never sit next to the same people. St. Anastasia uses the slogan to kick off a greeting at the beginning of Mass during which people turn and greet those beside them. "A couple weeks ago," Fr. Mech said, laughing, "two longtime families turned to each other, saying, 'Are you new here? Welcome to our parish!'" The enthusiastic welcome the parishioners give each other often has an even more powerful effect than a welcome from church staff or the pastor.

When parishioners start filing out of the church, vibrant parishes provide more for them than just a friendly goodbye wave. Some pastors encourage parishioners to stay behind by hosting a breakfast where people can get to know each other. Others prefer the classic coffee and donuts to accompany the long conversations that can take place outside the church after Mass.

It takes planning and work to create reasons for people to stick around and connect after Mass, which is part of what makes the Mass meaningful. Extending the power and joy of the Eucharist into the times and spaces before and after Mass allows some of the most important parishioner interactions to take place. "There's got to be joy, man, because people's lives are tough," says Fr. John Antony of Immaculate Conception in Fort Smith, Arkansas, who makes certain his parish provides regular times outside of Mass for people to be together. "They're hoping for someone to say, 'It's going to be okay. Jesus is going to help you through this. You're going to make it, and you're going to be better in the long run because you're walking with Christ.'" When the Sunday experience is left more to chance, it makes it all the more difficult for parishioners to find that human connection and solace in their worshiping.

ATTENDING TO CHILDREN

Many parents with infants find it very hard to bring them to Mass, especially if a toddler is also in tow. Single parents find it especially difficult. Children are an integral part of the Sunday experience, and they need to be accommodated. The goal of including children is two-fold: to support the spirituality of parents and to incorporate children into the community as soon as they are able.

Many of the churches we surveyed have recognized this and provide age-appropriate experiences for young children. These parishes identify the needs of each age level and strive to create a unique and attractive environment for them with furniture that fits their growing bodies, interesting and well-balanced programs, loving acceptance, and active involvement. Ultimately, these initiatives provide children with "time out" of the adult assembly for their own programming and then return them to join their families for "time in" during some portion of the regular Mass.

Usually, these parishes call the children up to the altar at the beginning of Mass and dismiss them for their "time out." They are led to a separate space for their own Liturgy of the Word, a homiletic experience designed for children. It is a presentation of the Gospel of the Sunday but simplified and more interactive. The children return to their families in the main church after the homily. Whether parishes call them Kids' Zones, Wee One's Words, or All Stars, these children's ministries offer great ways for both children and parents to get the most out of their Sunday experiences although they may be in separate rooms.

Children have "time in" when they are involved in the liturgy through music or other ministries. One pastor told us he is trying to build a kid-friendly liturgical atmosphere. Instead of focusing on the disturbance when children start crying, he focuses on using opportunities to engage them in the liturgy; for example, he invites them up to place the offerings in a basket during the offertory. Fr. William Hammer of St. Joseph Proto-Cathedral in Bardstown, Kentucky, commented that providing children's Masses that call for young cantors and readers brings the added benefit of drawing more parents and grandparents to Mass. "It's not intended to be a performance where you just watch kids sing," he said. "These kids are leading us in prayer and worship and liturgy. If it's the children singing, [the relatives] might only come Christmas and Easter, but they'll come."

PLANNING FOR A WELCOMING LITURGY

Roughly a quarter of our parishes (26.4 percent) are "destination parishes." These parishes are destinations in the sense that they draw attendance from multiple zip codes. People are willing to travel considerable distances to worship in these parishes, even crossing city and county lines and passing other churches to get there. Fr. J. Mark Hobson of Church of the Resurrection in Solon, Ohio, mentioned that parishioners drive by several Catholic parishes to arrive at Resurrection because of the parish's reputation for caring about the liturgy. Some pastors attributed their parishes' success to taking the liturgy seriously. But none of these liturgies happens without planning and effort.

"We're almost hyperorganized about the Sunday experience, especially the liturgy," one pastor in the Midwest explained. "That then means it all goes well, and it flows, and people aren't feeling uncomfortable. You know, one wrong note on an organ throws people—they stop singing. Or if it looks [as if] the servers are going to fall over, that distracts. We're not stiff, but there's a formality to it, there's an organization to it. People can feel comfortable, that 'Okay, they figured this out; we can enter into it.'" The confidence that a well-executed liturgy inspires in parishioners is critical to getting a Sunday experience off on the right foot.

Fr. Joseph Kempf of Assumption parish in O'Fallon, Missouri, who considers Sunday Mass the highlight of his week, spoke about the importance of liturgy: "Well-done liturgy deepens faith. It matters [that it] be done well. I care very much about that."

Significant planning—seasonally, weekly, morning-of—goes into setting up the Sunday worship experience so that it is engaging and dynamic (see figure 5.1). One of our pastors described how successful his liturgy committee is in helping the presiders, the deacons, the music team, and the RCIA team that meet once a week to plan the Sunday liturgy. They go over everything, including the scriptures, and begin developing a direction for the homily. Then they tie the music into all of it. Everything is planned weekly, and it is seasonally based. It is never off-the-cuff.

Some parishes have liturgical teams that get together to plan a series of homilies around one topic. In this way, the topic builds momentum from week to week. Ideally, each message builds on the one before, creating a sense of anticipation. A homily series can generate word-of-mouth advertising; people know exactly where a series is going and can look forward to the next installation.

HOSPITALITY BEGINS ONLINE AND IN THE ARCHITECTURE

Welcoming begins long before parishioners settle into the pews. It begins even before they make it to the parking lot. Hospitality means opening wide the doors, and the first portal of today's parish is its website. That's where Google directs strangers seeking a local Mass.

WELCOMING THROUGH TECHNOLOGY

Most of our parishes have highly effective websites. As is often the case, something done well is an inspiration to others to try it themselves. In one Parish Catalyst Learning Community,[3] which consisted of eleven pastors and their parish leadership teams, eight of the eleven parishes upgraded their websites during the eighteen-month period that they were members of the community.[4]

Figure 5.1 Planning the Sunday experience

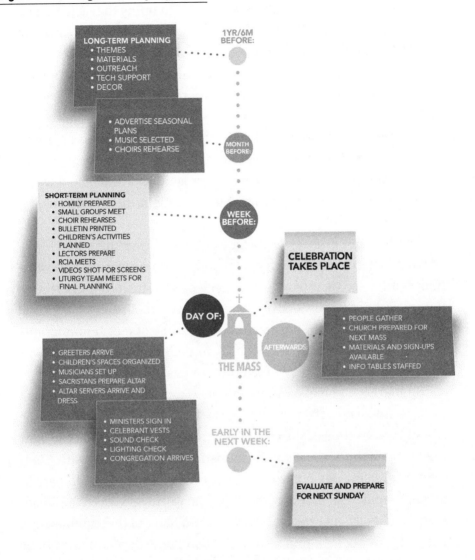

Parishes that understand technology as a critical tool for hospitality disseminate information through a range of platforms—including email, websites, Facebook, Twitter, podcasts, and blogs—in order to create the most coverage and impact. Parishes post readings, reflections, and pastors' blogs, along with updates on parish news and activities. Msgr. Charles Pope of Holy Comforter-St. Cyprian parish in

Washington, DC, publishes a blog that has an average of ten thousand visits every day. "I have a big pulpit there. I'm trying to reach out and do some work," he said. "I have been doing it for about five years, and the readership has grown pretty steadily. I put an article out almost every day." Additionally, every one of his Sunday homilies is available online in MP3 format for any of his five thousand Facebook friends to download.

For parishes that rely solely on lengthy and expensive paper bulletins, websites and online bulletins offer a practical alternative. Online bulletins provide information for parishioners who miss a weekend but still want to know what is happening in their parish before the next Sunday.

The Internet is a way to include people all over the world in the worship experience. Parishioners who travel for business and vacationers alike see their parish as a home base. A traveler can listen to the podcast of a homily delivered by her pastor in Boston from a hotel room in Beijing. When the daughter of a family of recent immigrants receives Confirmation, relatives back in their home country can witness the sacrament through the power of live streaming.

Similarly, a homebound parishioner can stay involved through these technologies. If she cannot come down the block in person, she can still feel as though she is participating in the Mass if she can view the liturgy online before the Eucharistic Minister arrives with Communion. Technology holds promise for including in worship parishioners from just about every region of the world and across all socioeconomic levels. As Fr. Ron Lewinski of St. Mary of the Annunciation parish in Mundelein, Illinois, put it, "You know they still want to be in touch with the parish somehow, so we have our homilies recorded and available on the website. There are new questions today. . . . When you start asking questions about what the Sunday attendance is or who's a regular or so forth, it's a little fuzzy in some ways because sometimes they're connected even though they're not here."

Parish websites need to include accurate and up-to-date information to welcome people to services and community activities hosted by the parish. The Mass schedule must be accessible online. If a parish can manage to maintain its schedule of Mass times and community-service and social-justice activities online, it encourages both parishioners and visitors to turn up and participate.

Once parishioners and guests find themselves in the church building, technology continues to help some parishes. "We're trying to be intentional about hospitality," says Fr. Steven Verhelst, who pastors four parishes that have come together as Catholic Area Faith Community of Jesus Our Living Water, in Willmar, Minnesota. Fr. Steven told us they began projecting prayers and hymn lyrics up on large screens at one of the churches in this community three years ago. "It quite literally has changed our celebration of the Sunday Eucharist. The change has just been incredible because of course people now are looking up rather than looking down in a hymnal."

When one parish renovated their church a few years ago, they installed large screens. Now, they broadcast the words across the screens and the parishioners sing out. Some parishes have done away with the songbook entirely in favor of screens.

INVITING GROUNDS AND ARCHITECTURE

One of the much older "technologies" parishes can use to welcome people to worship is their architecture. Both in its design and in its arrangement, a space can communicate a welcoming or an unwelcoming spirit. Yet, while more than 80 percent of the pastors we spoke to discussed their facilities and their architecture, only 10 percent appeared to connect the configuration of their architecture, their landscaping and grounds, or the maintenance of their facilities to their parishes' practices of welcoming.

Several pastors pointed to their parishes' attractive grounds and beautiful worship spaces as tools for invitation. For Fr. Leo Walsh of St. Benedict's in Anchorage, Alaska, healthy, well-kept grounds can express the health of the church they decorate: "Beautiful grounds are attractive to people wanting to come onto the property. . . . It feels [as if] these people care about their place." Fr. John Rice, who pastors St. Francis Xavier in Parkersburg, West Virginia, a church that is nearly

150 years old, remarked, "The church building itself is a source of pride for the community and an attraction to folks . . . whether they're Catholic or not." For Fr. Dan Schlegel at Holy Angels in Chagrin Falls, Ohio, his parish's sixty-four acres of uninhabited "beautiful" woods make their grounds more akin to a retreat center than a church. Said Fr. Schlegel, "When you drive in, you feel like you're leaving your worldly cares behind. I'm looking out of my office right now, and I can see no other buildings. All I see are leaves and deer."

A parish's local climate can determine where parishioners gather before Mass to socialize. Several of our parishes on the East Coast have large narthexes where greeters and parishioners gather when they arrive for worship.[5] Some of these front lobbies are social, loud, and bustling, whereas others have a solemn, toned-down atmosphere. At the opposite end of the spectrum and the country, Padre Serra parish in Camarillo, California, which has good weather year-round, has designed an outdoor gathering space in front of their church.

Churches in Chicago design indoor gathering spaces that encourage fellowship through all the seasons. Weather does not hold back the successful parishes we studied. "It's like a burst of Easter eggs when you walk into it," says Fr. Tom Hurley about the architecture of Chicago's Old St. Patrick's, built in 1856 by Irish immigrants. "The lighting, the interior—I think it's a sacred place. It really says something. It's very hopeful. It's helped in terms of our success."

The arrangement of interior spaces can promote a sense of community and connection among parishioners. Fr. Michael Saporito at St. Helen's in Westfield, New Jersey, says that there's a "very intimate, warm feel to the church. It's not a traditional setting. It's a three semicircle setting, but also the floor is slanted, and it has theater-style seating. When you preach, you really feel like you're in the people; it's got a unique feel."

Fr. T. Mathew Rowgh of St. Agnes in Shepherdstown, West Virginia, describes his parish's worship space as having two sides of seating facing each other. "The idea," he said, "was that we're a community gathered around the altar . . . so we're using the space in order to help people become aware of each other." Fr. Patrick Mullen's Padre Serra parish in Camarillo, California, achieves a similar effect with a worship space in the round. Said the pastor, "[The presence of the altar in the center] does so many things. The people notice each other. The center of attention isn't a priest down at the far end, with a bunch of backs of heads. The very architecture says 'we are in this together' . . . and 'you are the Church.' The architecture proclaims it: 'We're in this together, and we're gathered around that table, and we're on our way to the Lord together.'"

Even though the space can go a long way toward supporting the worship experience, it is possible to have a great liturgy in the absence of a magnificent space. In the case of St. Anthony on the Lake in Pewaukee, Wisconsin, the initial lack of a beautiful building was no hindrance to their community. In fact, it was quite the opposite. According to Fr. Tony Zimmer, parishioners used to meet "in that little basement church. There was an intimacy forged of relationships, of service, of care and kindness and generosity toward one another, and that core group of people is still here in this beautiful place of worship." The parish eventually grew and moved into a beautiful, open, and airy space, but Fr. Tony insists that the basement energy has remained intact: "They never left the basement. That same spirituality and intimacy is present."

Sometimes that communal effect can come from a worship space that is not permanent. One parish realigns the configuration of their church furniture, which is all movable—including their ambo and lectern—for various seasons and feast days. In this way the space remains fresh and newly engaging.

Of course, while a beautiful, well-designed church and grounds do attract initially, only the culture of hospitality and community within can keep people coming back. But it is valuable to consider what the visual impact of any church is on its Sunday experience and how using the space well can energize liturgy.

A PASTOR'S PRESENCE

The pastors we interviewed had a *personal* sense of hospitality. Pope Francis leads through example, and these pastors do the same. Their personal hospitality typically centers on presence: they are visible, prepared, and purposefully present during the Sunday experience as well as other moments in the life of the parish.

As one pastor said, there is no substitute for presence. Though his parish's excellent school is run by highly competent faculty and staff, he still makes sure he spends time there. Frequently, he walks over to the school without an agenda. He observes; he greets; he learns. This intentional practice of presence is, for him, the heart of his ministry.

Many pastors talked about making it a personal priority to be available to their parishioners: meeting people where they are, when they can—and being a "joyful presence to others." Fr. Michael Woods, pastor at All Saints parish in Knoxville, Tennessee, remarked, "My ministry certainly is servantly. . . . Every day, for me, it's [about,] how can I serve? How can I help?"

These pastors appreciate the weight that life's significant milestones (birth, marriage, death) carry and are intentional about being present for their parishioners during these times. Fr. Marcel Taillon, pastor of St. Thomas More parish in Narragansett, Rhode Island, said of his parishioners, "I feel very much like a father and very close to the people." Fr. Joseph Kempf of Assumption Church in O'Fallon, Missouri, remarked, "I minister a lot by presence. Anybody in the parish who has a loved one die . . . if I've not done the funeral or had a face-to-face, I will call every single one of those families to listen to them, ask them about their loved one, pray with them, and offer them the loving community and support of our parish."

In a similar vein, Msgr. John Barry of American Martyrs parish in Manhattan Beach, California, said his entire approach is presence: "I use the ministry of presence to the people—especially in crucial moments of their lives, the moments when they lose a family member or there's grave illness—to try to bring a spirit of openness and acceptance to people here. . . . My effort has always been to try to know my people and know their stories as fully as possible." Fr. Joseph Muth of St. Matthew's parish in Baltimore added, "It is a blessing to be able to walk with someone right up to the edge of life."

Like so many important pieces of the puzzle of parish life, the hospitality of a parish isn't a one-man job. The wise pastor looks at the people in the pews as a vast reserve of talent with great ministerial potential. The pastor who can light a fire within his current parishioners, inspiring them not only to create room for new parishioners but to develop their own faith though involvement in parish hospitality, can truly impact a community both inside and outside the parish. His presence as pastor, kind shepherd, is crucial on all levels of parish life.

PREACHING TAKES A *LOT* OF TIME

Parishes with a great Sunday experience have pastors who enjoy preaching and spend a lot of time preparing for it. For pastors who enjoy preaching, it's about far more than merely standing up and speaking for its own sake; they have something to say. "From my chair, the preaching is all-important," says Fr. Jeffrey Nicolas of the Cathedral of the Assumption in Louisville, Kentucky. "So the preparation and the encounter that people have through the preaching are there." Agreeing with Fr. Nicolas is St. Agnes's Fr. Matthew Rowgh in Shepherdstown, West Virginia, who insists that a significant amount of pastors' time and energy goes into preparing ahead of time to preach.

No matter how good a pastor's intentions, without devoting enough time and energy to preparation, he might be too thinly spread to consider ways to improve his preaching. To parishioners, the difference between pastors well prepared to preach and those who aren't able to make time is as clear as night and day. Fr. Kevin Anderson of Christ Our Light parish in Princeton, Minnesota, summed it up perfectly: "If you go up to a Catholic, any Catholic on the street, and say, 'Tell me about your priest,' inevitably they're going to talk about his preaching. Maybe later on they'll talk about his bedside manner or his finances or something, but almost always it's 'Oh, he's dynamic,' or 'He's pretty boring, but he's a nice guy.' For our guys, that should be the most important thing you work on all week."

Many pastors commented on the enjoyment they derive from preaching. Fr. Paul Duchschere of Sts. Anne and Joachim parish in Fargo, North Dakota, remarked: "That's the funny thing about being a priest. I'm like everybody else; just like everyone else, I get tired of things after a while. But I've never gotten tired of Mass. I've never gotten tired of offering Mass and offering a homily. Never. It's one of the greatest blessings in my life."

FINDING THE TIME

Developing a homily takes prayer, preparation, and practice. One rule of thumb suggests that every minute of a homily takes an hour of preparation. By that measure, a ten-minute homily takes ten hours to develop. Parishes with a great Sunday experience have pastors who enjoy preaching and are disciplined about finding the time they require for preparation. "Now that I'm getting a little more seasoned, I could probably spend, I would say, half an hour [preparing] for every minute that I preach," says Fr. Dan Swift of St. Benedict's parish in Holmdel, New Jersey. "My homilies are about seven to eight minutes, so that's about four hours."

With the distractions and commitments that most pastors have, finding five to ten hours a week to work on a homily may seem to be an impossible task. The only way a pastor can accomplish it is to have time set aside when he is not disturbed; this may require that staff and volunteers take over some of the opening prayers at meetings, meetings themselves, and drop-by visits. In order for the pastor to be able to concentrate on homily creation, not only do staff and parishioners need to accept that a meeting is just as valid and a prayer just as sacred without Father but the pastor himself must release control and trust those who do the ministerial work.

FINDING INSPIRATION

Where do pastors look for ideas for their homilies? Although we found no consensus on where the content and inspiration for good homilies come from, the short answer is absolutely everywhere. Fr. Bob Tabbert of St. John XXIII parish in Fort Myers, Florida, tries to include an anonymized story of a particular parishioner to personalize the homilies as much as he can for his audience. Meanwhile, at Holy Trinity parish in Louisville, Kentucky, Fr. Mark Spalding scours the Internet for insights, ideas, and topics. "I just type whatever topic into YouTube," he says, jazzed about the abundance of preaching resources online. "They have these fifteen-minute TED presentations. Oh, my gosh!" Fr. Joseph Kempf at Assumption parish in O'Fallon, Missouri, infuses his preaching with self-reflection and stories about his own life. "I look back on my life and go, 'Well, it was a life well lived,'" he says. "I was well used, and I offer my gift. Just to get to be a part of something that matters—I am so grateful for that."

These pastors are curious and creative. They seek wide-ranging input. They draw inspiration from conversations with fellow clergy, from talking with and reading the perspectives of religious thinkers, from listening to the homilies and sermons of others online. Conferences on topics from evangelization to stewardship to religious education (only some of which are specifically Catholic) are sources of inspiration as well.

The pastors we interviewed tend to be voracious readers with eclectic tastes. Popular Catholic texts included *America* magazine, *National Catholic Reporter*, the writings of Pope Francis, Michael White and Tom Corcoran's *Rebuilt*, Matthew Kelly's *The Four Signs of a Dynamic Catholic*, and Sherry Weddell's *Forming Intentional Disciples*. However, materials by evangelicals were also on the pastors' lists of recommended reading, especially Rick Warren's books *The Purpose Driven Life* and *The Purpose Driven Church* and other materials from the evangelical Christian megachurches Saddleback (founded by Warren) and Willow Creek Community Church (founded by Bill Hybels). We did not speak to any pastor who created his homilies using only one source.

When asked where they looked for new ideas for their homilies, a surprising 31 percent shared that their own Catholic faith was enhanced by the inspiration they found in non-Catholic sources. Fr. James Mallon of St. Benedict Church in Halifax, Nova Scotia, remarked: "I have many contacts in the evangelical world, locally, that I touch base with. I have a very strong connection with Alpha International . . . not just as a parish force [but] as an entire philosophy of renewal and leadership, and so I am a member of the International Board of Alpha in a Catholic Context. I read Bill Hybels and read Rick Warren [and] found them very inspiring."

The roots of ecumenical influence were deep in some cases, stretching back to seminary training and even childhood. Fr. John Riccardo of Our Lady of Good Counsel parish in Plymouth, Michigan, said that his family of origin embraced multiple faiths: "I came from a mixed family, in terms of faith, growing up. My mother was Methodist; my dad was Catholic. My mom's Catholic now, but I have three sisters who are all evangelicals. My brother's Catholic. And so I . . . grew up in a family that was what [George] Weigel calls 'evangelically Catholic.' That was my family, which has been helpful in the sense of pastoring because I was taught a lot of things from my siblings and my parents that were really helpful for guiding people to the faith."

Fr. Jeffrey Nicolas of Assumption Cathedral in Louisville, Kentucky, described a seminary training that extended beyond Catholicism: "I've studied at the Southern Baptist Seminary for some courses during seminary time. I went to the Presbyterian seminary. I've got a very ecumenical background, and I've come out of the whole thing stronger in my Catholicism—and again, not a defensiveness and not a cliquishness but just a confidence. And so . . . I don't misstep much when dealing with the city or dealing with the other faiths." Exposure to other faiths during formative periods of their lives has strengthened the Catholic faith of these two pastors and helped them show compassion for and connect with a broader range of people. Since a preacher must connect with his audience, their backgrounds assist them in delivering meaningful homilies.

Some pastors were explicit in recommending a more Protestant approach to homilies. Fr. Bob Campbell of Our Lady of the Most Holy Rosary parish in Albuquerque, New Mexico, said, "I don't give homilies; I preach sermons. . . . I would describe my preaching style as dynamic, not reading the homily but speaking directly to the people, and I would describe it as a Protestant style of preaching. And I would add that I think Catholic pastors have much to learn from our evangelical and Protestant brother and sister ministers, in terms of preaching styles and being able to connect with people, and so that's what I try to do."

Along the same lines, Fr. Tom Connery of St. Peter's Church in DeLand, Florida, remarked: "Well, I still look at Rick Warren, [though] sometimes I get a little overwhelmed by the expansive ministries, and Willow Creek Community Church—the leadership development that they have. I get their monthly CD and listen to it, and that has helped me a lot, especially Bill Hybels. He's very strong on leadership. Andy Stanley as well—I listen to his podcast, his workshops. And then my local Catholic priests—I listen to their homilies, go to their websites. All over the diocese, I like to know what they're doing, read about them." For this respondent (and many others like him), the evangelical models offered by the spectacularly successful Willow Creek Community Church fruitfully inform homily preparations right alongside resources from brother priests within the Catholic faith.

Perhaps Msgr. Pablo Navarro of St. John Neumann parish in Miami, Florida, sums up the wide-ranging and inclusive omnivorous approach best. When asked about where he looks for inspiration for his homilies, Msgr. Navarro answered, "Anywhere. I am a thief. Any idea that I see, anywhere, that is working—I have no shame. I will ask. I will go to Protestants, to the neighboring synagogue, to the imam. I will pick everybody's brain, including my brother priests'." Again, nearly one in three of the pastors in our dataset spoke animatedly about engaging with ideas from other religious traditions.

GAUGING SUCCESS

In her book *Connecting Pulpit and Pew*, Karla Bellinger writes, "I learned that preaching is a deeply sensitive subject. I discovered that listeners hunger for inspiration; they want to hear a message that gives them life. Clergy told me that they thirst for their people to encounter Jesus Christ; they want to inspire their people; they want to see the fruit of a Christian life. I also heard undercurrents of frustration on both sides."[6]

Enthusiastic homilies that are prepared and delivered well can have a telling impact on a parish's health. One of the biggest drivers for parishioners to recommend their parish to someone else is the pastor and his preaching.[7] Yet these inspired, well-prepared homilies are not always met with enthusiasm. Responding to a question about what the liturgy is like at his parish, Fr. Carl Diederichs of All Saints parish in Milwaukee, Wisconsin, said, "A lot of hand clapping, a lot of response even to my homilies. When it's just a regular homily, I don't get any applause. But when I do strike a chord, I always get applause after a homily. But it's good that it's not always because there are some times when you're just not 'on' as much as you are other times. . . . And when they don't do it, I say, 'That's fine.' I didn't come to expect applause, but when you get it, you say, 'Well, they must have heard something.'" Fr. Diederichs is candid about the reality that not every homily is equally insightful or inspiring. He relies on his congregation to give him feedback, and because applause is not guaranteed, he can actually trust it.

A successful homily presentation can depend a great deal on how well the pastor can deal with distractions. Fr. Michael Woods of All Saints parish in Knoxville, Tennessee, remarked, "I try to be very child-friendly. Sometimes you might have a roaring child right in the middle of the homily when you want to preach, and you feel the tension, but you say, 'Wow, do you hear that child crying?' And I'll . . . leave where I am and go down and pick up the child and use them in my homily in one way or another. Calms everybody down. So I try to be child-friendly, and I know parents have a hard time."

While neither pastors nor parishes can control the way parishioners will receive homilies, the information we collected from pastors suggests that allocating significant preparation time and investigating a range of material increase the likelihood that a homily will resonate with the people in the pews.

MORE THAN SOUND AND WORDS

Vibrant music is essential to the vibrant liturgies celebrated in the parishes of this study. Nearly half of the pastors named their liturgical music as one of the greatest assets of their parish. Anyone who has been moved while singing a hymn, a psalm, or praise music knows at an intuitive level that something more than sound and words has touched them. "The music obviously touches a deep chord in people's lives here," said Fr. George Schopp of Our Lady of Grace parish in Chicago, Illinois. "It fills the Masses, and they respond. And it's tremendous being in a church with about 600 to 800 people who are singing. They're blowing the roof off the place! I can't imagine things being—how can it get better? And there's a genuineness about it."

Good music, however it is presented, can spark an intensely emotional response. Parishes with strong music programs are exceptional at fostering this component of the Sunday experience. Another pastor saw a drastic change in his parish when they took their music program to the next level:

> A couple hundred years ago, we needed hymns that were didactic, that taught us the faith. But I don't need hymns like that so much now; I need hymns that help me express my love for Jesus. So we're trying to find a way to blend all that. So we offer different styles. The point of music in a church isn't to get Father from A to B. The point of music is to break open your heart so that the Word can get planted inside of it. So we're trying to always have worship that enables that to happen.

Planting the Word is possible without music, but it is more difficult and depends even more heavily on good preaching.

NO ONE STYLE FITS ALL

Worship music has become diversified. Along with the traditional hymns, chants, and classical Latin Mass settings, contemporary liturgical music aims to provide a direct and meaningful style of worship music. Some dislike the newer music, which they believe makes the participation of the assembly too high a priority and discounts the spiritual aesthetic that characterized earlier sacred music. Others find the newer music revitalizing to their faith. Striking a balance between the various styles of music and the various musical sensibilities of parishioners has become a tricky prospect for many parish teams.

Strong parish music programs are populated with singers, instrumentalists, and directors who are strong musicians and strong worship leaders. Getting the best musical talent the parish can find and afford is a priority for our pastors. One pastor from a major Midwestern city told us that the genuineness of his Sunday experience depends on whether his parishioners are singing along to the music. What matters is attention to the music. The common threads are effort, budgetary investment, and talented staff and volunteers with sufficient time.

There are parishes out there with undeniably fantastic music programs. Fr. Jerry Kaywell, who was a Grammy winner himself with Quincy Jones in 1987, made music a priority at Sacred Heart parish in Punta Gorda, Florida, when he arrived and saw that it needed some work. "I made sure that the sound and light system is killer. It's state-of-the-art. We have 180 speakers in surround sound for the Rodgers Trillium organ. We have a Schimmel eight-foot-four-inch grand piano and all the synthesizers and cool stuff," he said, before moving on to the quality of the music itself. "If it were any better, we'd be at performance levels, which would distract from the liturgy, so it's just right. I would say our music is perfect."

The pastors we spoke to emphasized that spending time and energy to find out what worked best for their parish was an important step on the path to a successful music program. Even though music requires time, staff, energy, and budget, there is no one-size-fits-all approach.

Today there is such a multitude of musical forms that it is hard to classify them at all. People create their own playlists, write and post their own music on social-media websites, and prefer different musical styles. Taste in sacred music, like taste in other forms of music and prayer, is eclectic and personal.

There is no optimal type or style of liturgical music. The strong music ministries in our sample were diverse and mixed. One Midwestern parish exhibited a huge range in their music: one weekend it was contemporary, two weeks before that it was Celtic, the next week it was more traditional. For some parishes, a great music program can mean having a bit of everything within the same Mass. One parish favors a blend of Gregorian chant and spirituals from the African American tradition. Both the type of music and how that music is made were unique to each vibrant parish we surveyed.

A Wisconsin pastor said, "And then, in terms of the music, I think that we offer a variety of music. We keep great instrumentation, great-trained cantors, and a variety of different choirs—contemporary ensemble, traditional, bells—and all those different things like that. We also try to incorporate a lot of the young people in that. We have a lot of the Millennials who are cantors; we have instrumentalists who do all that."

A pastor from New Jersey remarked, "[We] talk with our music ministers all the time about keeping stuff good and vibrant and upbeat and new. And I have to say my music ministers are great at that. They bring me a lot more stuff than I bring to them, but we talk about it a lot."

Instrumentation can range from pipe organs to guitars to drums with varying effects. One parish we spoke with has a marvelous music ministry with modern, lively music featuring electric guitar, bass, and keyboards that is very effective without having much in the way of formality. Another parish uses piano, organ, flutes, violins, and drums alongside tambourines and various Hawaiian instruments such as rain sticks. Fr. Shay Auerbach, S.J., at Sacred Heart parish in Richmond, Virginia, mentioned that a trumpet makes an appearance at his Spanish-language Masses.

Some parishes are known for an international and multicultural approach to music. In addition to having an English-language Mass featuring gospel music, they have multilingual choirs. Two parishes we spoke to invite Kenyan, Sudanese, Nigerian, Cameroonian, and Filipino choirs to perform at their Sunday Masses a few times every year. Other parishes have the same music at each weekend service, which is pleasing to parishioners who appreciate consistency, unity, and coordination across Masses.

Above all, no matter which Mass they attend, parishioners like to know what they are going to get in advance. And whatever the style and instrumentation, it is essential that the music be locally sensitive. Whether it is bringing in a marimba player the parish loved for the Christmas Mass or inviting a vocal group in to make the music more harmonious, our parishes work at developing music programs that resonate with the people they serve.

EQUIPMENT AND TALENT

Wherever a parish falls on the music diversity spectrum, having professional gear and a professional staff is enormously helpful. Parishes with extraordinary music programs make it a priority. Heavy investment of both energy and talent are necessary in order for a music program to excel. That does not mean parishes have to break the bank; instead more energy may need to be spent finding musicians. If local high schools and colleges boast strong music programs of their own, parishes can try to attract music majors and members of the marching band as did one parish we spoke to in a small town in the Midwest. That added effort can help develop a vibrant Sunday music experience, whether the parish has a healthy music budget or not.

If funds can be made available, sound systems and screens are expensive but appear substantially to enhance the worship experience at the parishes where they are implemented. While parishes use talented volunteers if they are available, many parishes pay their cantors and musicians, and one parish reported paying both their main keyboard player and their choir leader seventy-five dollars per Mass. They are trained to do what they do, and the impact they have is evident every Sunday.

The importance of having the right person in the role of director of music cannot be overstated. According to Fr. Tom Lilly, St. Elizabeth Ann Seton parish in Anchorage, Alaska, was lucky to find a music director right there in their pews. He was a jazz pianist by training and had spent twenty-two years in the Air Force band. At Christ Our Light parish in Cherry Hill, New Jersey, Fr. Tom Newton held a national search to find a director capable of collaborating with the parish in developing the popular worship experience they enjoy today. Music directors can be pivotal in helping parishes determine exactly what the goal for their music program is and how best to use the parish space to achieve it.

The pastor's presence and leadership may seem too obvious to mention, but they are essential to a parish's sense of community and well-being. The sacred synergy of intentional hospitality, inspirational preaching, and high-quality music makes Mass relevant in people's lives.

All these components are the recurring characteristics in the hundreds of islands of strength and mercy that we encountered. If there is fresh-baked bread inside an American Catholic parish and a welcome sign proclaiming it, the hungry will come forward and be richly fed.

CRUCIAL TAKEAWAYS

1. Vibrant, welcoming Sunday liturgies require thorough staff planning and a well-organized network of volunteer ministers. Seventy-six percent of the pastors we interviewed identified this as a crucial strength of their parishes.

2. Attention to the needs of the children in the community is a critical success factor for vibrant parishes.

3. Hospitality begins with a parish's online presence, which must be kept fresh and relevant to the expressed needs of both parishioners and newcomers.

4. The physical plant's upkeep and suitability to meet the needs of the worshiping community are key factors in creating a vibrant worship experience.

5. Flourishing parishes have pastors who love being present to their people and who are highly disciplined about setting aside long hours of time and attention for homily preparation.

6. Music is central to the Sunday experience. Significant time, talent, equipment, and money must be budgeted in order to deliver great liturgical music.

6

—

CHALLENGES TO EXCELLENT SUNDAYS

The greatest opportunity is that there is tremendous spiritual yearning among people in general. We have the answer to that yearning. We have Jesus Christ, crucified, resurrected from the dead, in the Eucharist, in the Body and Blood, that can feed people spiritually, and I believe that if we can bring people who are spiritually seeking, who have an emptiness in their life, who are wondering, "Is this all there is?" then we can help them connect with God.

—Fr. Bob Campbell
Our Lady of the Most Holy Rosary, Albuquerque, New Mexico

While hospitality, homilies, and hymns create the atmosphere for vibrant worship, they only lay the groundwork. The most critical component of all is the community of people in attendance. Fr. Michael Ryan of St. James Cathedral in Seattle, Washington, addressed this specifically: "I would love to overcome the Catholic malaise about Mass attendance. I think it's a national thing, and we do pretty well, but I don't think we do well enough."

There is a perspective shift at the end of that quotation. It is a subtle shift, but one that can make all the difference: "I don't think we do well enough." That sentiment represents a viewpoint shared by many of our pastors. It lifts the sole blame for lack of attendance off the shoulders of the parishioner and invites a parish leadership team to take an honest look at the parish's strategies for the Sunday experience. The question changes from "Why don't people come to Mass anymore?" to "Are we providing what people need from church?"

This chapter addresses the most common stumbling blocks to dynamic worship: a secular culture in which church is all too often perceived as just one of many weekend "options," a change in the culture away from religious affiliation, parishioners' inflexibility and resistance to change, and difficulty with new technologies. Despite these challenges, there are good reasons to be optimistic and clear avenues for improving the Sunday experience specifically through understanding attitudes toward attendance, embracing change in parish structure and culture, and making better use of digital media.

A CULTURE OF BUSYNESS

When the pastors we interviewed spoke about the challenges they encounter with the Sunday experience, they sometimes vented frustrations about parishioners' not coming to Mass on Sundays by mentioning the word "laziness." This single, undesirable label oversimplifies a complicated situation. As with most easy answers to important questions, there is something bigger at play behind this "laziness."

Harvard economist Juliet B. Schor, in her 1992 book *The Overworked American*, wrote that "the average employed person is now on the job an additional 163 hours, or the equivalent of an extra month a year," compared to figures for 1969. Dr. Schor estimated that US manufacturing employees work 320 hours more than their French or German counterparts annually. This equates to two months per year. Work and creativity increase when workers are rested. But leisure time, or time for recreation (re-creation) is no longer a given in many American lives, and when taken, it can come with a cost.

Whether practicing Catholics are temporarily or chronically burned out from working, raising children, or simply navigating their weekly life load, Sunday morning may be the only time of the week when they have any control over their own time. With depleted energy and coping reserves, they sometimes allow rest to trump religion.

Beyond the need for rest there is also the prevailing busyness factor. Until very recently, Sunday was considered a day of rest in the Western world. But now Sunday, church, and rest are in competition with a variety of other priorities.

Pastors were anxious to understand what exactly was keeping people away from Mass on Sunday. According to Fr. Michel Mulloy, the people of the Cathedral of Our Lady of Perpetual Help in Rapid City, South Dakota, work up to twelve-hour days, leaving them with little time to spend involved in a church. He added, "I think there's an underlying fear that 'If my kids aren't busy, they're going to get in trouble, and so I want to keep them involved in wholesome, healthy activities, and sports provides an easy way to do that.'" Fr. Mulloy has watched sports go from a healthy recreational distraction to an all-encompassing affair: "What initially might be identification of talent that a child has becomes almost an expectation that they will develop that talent and [a] hope that they will get a scholarship." Also, parishes in affluent communities witness flux, as parishioners travel extensively for both work and leisure.

Work, kids, travel, exercise—do these busy factors sound familiar? The reality is that just about anything can distract a parishioner from making Sunday Mass attendance a priority. What can parishes do to cut through the busyness and lift Mass above the many competing options on a Sunday morning? We found that many pastors viewed this challenge as a wake-up call to improve parish practices to meet the needs of the people.

Before we answer that question, let's look a little deeper at what's keeping people away.

THE STATISTICS OF SECULARITY

The Pew Research Center estimates that "13% of all Americans are former Catholics—people who no longer identify with the faith despite having been raised in the Catholic Church."[1] Fifty-nine percent of those raised Catholic still identify with Catholicism as adults; 41 percent do not.[2]

Even as immigration keeps American Catholicism vigorous in the near term, trends suggest that by the third generation, many of the descendants of immigrants will have left the Catholic faith. According to a Pew Research study released in May 2014, the proportion of US Latinos and Hispanics who identify as Catholic dropped from 67 percent to 55 percent in the five years prior. Approximately 25 percent of Latinos and Hispanic Americans are now themselves part of the "lapsed Catholic" group,[3] and the slump is most pronounced among those who are college-educated Millennials.[4] There is no single cause behind these changes, but scholars consider the rising influence of evangelicals in Latin America and the rising secularity in American culture as probable factors. The Pew study found that the majority of the Hispanic Americans who had left the Church had left Christianity altogether. In most cases, they said that they had simply stopped believing Church doctrine. Of those who had converted to Protestant denominations, however, roughly half said they had left because "they found a congregation that reaches out and helps its members more than the [Catholic] Church."[5] In other words, these young Latino and Hispanic people are not leaving because they prefer the more entertaining liturgies of a church down the street; they leave because they find their spiritual needs better met elsewhere.

All Christian denominations are facing attrition. It seems that each new survey shows a larger number of people in this country who are unaffiliated with any religious group. As Isaac Chotiner wrote in *New Republic*, despite high levels of religiosity in the United States, "popular culture, education, and politics operate within an essentially secular paradigm."[6] According to a 2015 Pew study, "The percentage of Americans who are religiously unaffiliated—describing themselves as atheist, agnostic or 'nothing in particular'—has jumped more than six points, from 16.1% [in 2007] to 22.8% [in 2014]."[7] The population of religious "nones" is growing.

Some contend that fewer people are turning away from the faith than these statistics suggest: perhaps it is simply the case that Americans are more prepared to identify as agnostic or atheist than they have been in the past. A 2012 Pew article reported that 60 percent of those surveyed in 2007 who said they seldom or never attended religious services nonetheless claimed a particular religious affiliation. By 2012, only 50 percent of that same group still retained a religious affiliation.[8] The same Pew survey reports that in 2012, 37 percent of Americans thought of themselves as being "spiritual" but not "religious," a category that many, both within and outside of Christianity, have struggled to dissect and define.[9] In short, though many Americans still identify with a religion or with a more general spirituality, we are less concerned with religious affiliation than the previous generation.[10]

Aware of this shifting tide, our pastors look for ways to draw parishioner interest with events and topics that support their daily lives in the secular world.[11]

RESISTANCE TO NEEDED CHANGE

Drawing the interest of today's over stimulated parishioner back to a vibrant Sunday experience can require dramatic changes. Perhaps the Mass times no longer suit the parish population. Perhaps a new music program needs to be incorporated. These changes can require more than creative effort; they can require change in the way staff members or loyal parishioners experience their roles in the community. Our pastors reported that sometimes the greatest barrier to change in parish life is a member of the parish staff or a group of parishioners whose comfortable routine would be disrupted. This proved to be especially true if a proposed change would impact either the worship space or the liturgy itself. Those disenchanted with a change should be heard but should not be allowed to prevent needed changes from taking place.

One pastor spoke about a competence issue he had with the parish music director: "The music was pitiful—generally off key and out of tune. She did the best she could but she really didn't have much to work with. The problem of addressing the music under her leadership was complicated because she was so nice. She would do anything for anybody." A natural disaster came through and destroyed this church's musical equipment. The music director was out of town on vacation during the disaster and asked what would happen. The pastor simply told her he had to start from scratch. Someone new took over, and by the time the old music director returned, she got the message. While it was not exactly a "firing" per se, the pastor had released a troublesome staff member.

Sometimes long-standing negative behaviors on a parish staff or in a volunteer position are permitted to continue. There are times when a person needs to move on and let someone new minister, and there are times when ministerial roles can be restructured to make a parish professional or volunteer team more productive.

Often the change is more of a push and pull between parishioners and the parish leadership. One pastor in the Northeast said, "Right now the church does not have a permanent baptismal font, and so I have proposed building one; I think it's pretty important. And a lot of folks think that's a good idea, and a lot of folks don't think it's a good idea. That's been a point of contention."

Communicating the need for specific changes before they occur helps reduce tensions. Comments about changes where parishioners had no buy-in can ring through the minds of pastors long afterward, as they do for one small-town pastor. He can easily recall cries of "You took away my Mass!" Comments such as these are at once inspiring and disheartening: inspiring because they exhibit parishioners' deep sense of ownership and passion for their worship space but disheartening in that some parishioners are unable to see that the change may well provide new people a greater opportunity to worship with them.

Even when parishes are able to take the time and plan well for change to their Sunday experience, things do not always go as planned. Nowhere is this more apparent than with changes to music programs. Having music at all can send certain parishioners for the exits. "We had a number of people leave because they didn't want music," says a pastor from the Midwest. "Part of worship is music. Part of music is praise. And so we're going to have an opening and closing, and we're going to sing the psalm refrain. A number of people didn't like that."

With many parishes moving toward contemporary liturgical music, it comes as no surprise that those who prefer the more traditional hymnody can be dissatisfied with the change. When a suburban parish in the South introduced more upbeat, popular songs, many parishioners simply stopped singing.

The best intentions can be met with parishioner disapproval. A pastor in the Northeast reached out to invite the large Sudanese community in his parish to participate musically. The drums and traditional African rhythms joined a preexisting choir accustomed to performing classical and Latin hymns. He continues to be enthusiastic about the parish's diverse liturgy but admits that some parishioners have moved on to other churches because of the change.

Whether introducing a change in the Mass schedule, the style of music, or personnel, parish leadership should be straightforward with parishioners and continue to move the parish in the direction they have discerned to be best for the parish as a whole. Committing to the development of an exceptional Sunday liturgy will require change for many parishes. And some time generally must pass before changes are digested in full by the parish.

TECH TROUBLES

Many parishes have plenty of room for improvement of their Sunday experience in the area of technology. Pastors said that limitations of time and expertise have made it challenging to use technologies to the extent they would like. Even the most vibrant parishes are still trying to wrap their arms around the potential of new technologies.

Among our respondents, only 16.8 percent named technology and social media as strengths of their parishes, which means that these areas did not occur to 83.2 percent when they reflected on the strengths of their parish. Approximately 16 percent of interviewees listed technology and social media as emerging opportunities for growth—areas where pastors hope for improvement. Finally, 10.9 percent view technology and social media as an ongoing and difficult challenge. There appears to be enormous room for growth and development here (see figure 6.1).

Surprisingly very few of the pastors we interviewed mentioned technology or social media as important to their ministry. Today these are critical avenues of communication, important ways to inform people about almost everything.

Some parishes want to update, or gather for the first time, the email addresses of their parishioners in order to communicate with them efficiently when there is an important announcement to share. Others want to blog or make use of Facebook. Most parishes today have a website, but many have not as yet committed time and talent to the ongoing attention required to keep a website engaging and informative enough to draw visitors. One of the pastors interviewed admitted that he knows his parish website has a lot of room to grow, but the days go by without anyone there to improve it.

Though most parishes have accepted the digitization of American life, the abundance of new technologies is complicated and difficult to manage. Too few pastors appreciate the potential of technology for

Figure 6.1 Pastors and technology

PASTORS SAW THE USE OF TECHNOLOGY IN THEIR PARISH AS:

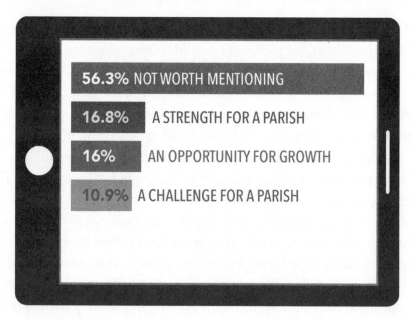

56.3% NOT WORTH MENTIONING

16.8% A STRENGTH FOR A PARISH

16% AN OPPORTUNITY FOR GROWTH

10.9% A CHALLENGE FOR A PARISH

communicating information to parishioners about the parish's activities and worship, but sometimes even the most basic elements go missing. "I don't even think the Mass schedule is on there," admitted one pastor, explaining the difficulty he is having with a newly hired website design firm. Some pastors confessed to having no idea what is actually on the parish website, and one pastor candidly confessed, "Our website now is a wreck."

Tech trouble can come at the most inconvenient times for parishes. A pastor in Arkansas had the misfortune of having his parish's website crash the week of Ash Wednesday. "It was terrible," the pastor said. "People are trying to find Mass times so they can get their ashes. I just had to apologize and say, 'We're trying to fix it.'"

Beyond the basics, there are always photos to be uploaded, new ministries to be added, and schedules to be released, but finding tech-savvy help is a major issue for pastors. Many pastors realize they need somebody with the right abilities if they want to reach younger people through new media. Often pastors find themselves on the wrong side of the generation gap when it comes to high-tech leaps. "As a sixty-seven-year-old pastor, I need somebody that is younger who can be by my side that can maybe start some sort of a high-tech communication thing," said Fr. Henry Petter of St. Ann parish in Coppell, Texas. "That's just not me." Msgr. Doug Cook of Holy Family Cathedral in Orange, California, admitted that technology is a personal shortcoming of his: "I don't take to it well. The social connection media, I haven't gotten into it. That's a lapse in my skill set." For other pastors, the budget is simply not there for them to do everything with technology that they would like to do.

Our pastors indicated that liturgical technology requires patience; and even when the budget and the personnel are there, the technology should not overshadow the liturgy. Opinion can be divided on the best way for a parish to move forward with liturgical technology. "We have a couple of evangelical megachurches that use a lot of technology and big screens," said Fr. Wayne Pittard of St. Pius X parish in

Billings, Montana. "Some say, 'That should be what we have,' in the sense of almost a show-type thing instead of time for prayer."

Despite the challenges, there is great potential to improve the Sunday experience with technology. "What kind of equipment do we need so we can start broadcasting the liturgy?" wondered Fr. James Cink of St. Dominic parish in Mobile, Alabama. "I have an associate who's better at it than me. He films his homilies and posts them on the web." This pastor is also working to accommodate his seniors using an infrared sound system so they can hear the liturgy more clearly.

Embracing the opportunities that come from improved technology means turning to the right people for the job. Many pastors are embracing technology the way they do any other challenge: with help from their staff. "You're not going to get a blog out of me," said Msgr. Mark Svarczkopf of Our Lady of the Greenwood parish in Greenwood, Indiana, chuckling. "But the stewardship development guy has a blog." Elsewhere, at St. Ann parish in Marietta, Georgia, Fr. Tom Reilly reported that his parish stepped into a technology opening and is now thriving: "We have a little recording studio where we make our own videos. The guy that does it is extremely creative. A few minutes before Mass we'll show the video. For Mother's Day the video was very clever. Anyone could send in a picture of their mother, and at the end we had it so that all the pictures formed an image of Mary and the Christ Child." According to the pastors we interviewed, there will always be special people to add that special touch. It might not come right away, but testing technology out will eventually lead to tangible benefits.

Even as parishes ratchet up their technology use, there continues to be room for improvement. To date, the function of technologies for these pastors seem to be mostly unidirectional, focused on dispersing information. Their potential as two-way communicative devices or forums for community participation is not being fully realized. For example, smartphone-based apps were not mentioned as components of tech initiatives, although parishioners are using apps prominently in their daily lives. Parishes could potentially benefit a great deal from embracing such aspects of social media. Currently, only a handful of the pastors consider this next stage of interactive technology as a core component of their ministry.

More than technology or other services, successful parishes depend on effective liturgies that touch people. "A lady approached me this morning and said, 'Father, I sat in church on Sunday totally touched by that unbelievable liturgy. It just touched my soul,'" recounted Msgr. Liam Kidney of Corpus Christi Church in Pacific Palisades, California. "We make efforts to try to make sure that what's happening is somehow real for these people." Prioritizing the Sunday experience will create opportunities for more worshipers to have similar epiphanies.

CHALLENGES RECAPPED

1. There are a great many competing priorities that keep people from worship and community on any given Sunday.

2. The population of religious "nones" continues to swell in the United States.

3. Changes often create tension, especially those that involve changing a liturgical style or the worship space.

4. Parishes suffer when people who hinder forward movement are allowed to continue in leadership roles.

5. Communication technologies are very underused in most parishes. Their potential for two-way communication and helping to build community participation is rarely richly realized.

PART IV

GREAT PARISHES EVANGELIZE

GETTING TO KENYA

Have you heard the slogan "attraction not promotion"? My pastor never pressures people about getting involved in the parish, but it is hard not to be attracted to him and to the ministries offered at St. Monica's. There is so much you can do. Among the opportunities are the parish missions.

I have done a fair amount of traveling with Msgr. Torgerson and always enjoy doing so, in no small part because he is full of energy and it's just fun to be with him. Once, he was gearing up to do a missionary trip to Kenya. I had some extra time, so I asked him, "Is there room for me to jump on?"

"Definitely," he said.

Nairobi is a bustling Kenyan city, and there are certain parts that are very poor. We traveled to our sister parish in nearby Dandora. The poverty was unlike anything I had ever seen before. The neighborhood was also home to the city's largest garbage dump. Right next door to our sister parish, I watched people scrounge for food in huge piles of rubbish—a sight both humbling and heartbreaking. Although we didn't work, we provided funds for their school expansion and met the many children who would benefit from the educational opportunity. There are, of course, many different ways to evangelize; certainly one way is to support the evangelization efforts of others.

When I returned to the sanctuary of St. Monica's after that trip, I understood how lucky we are to engage in missionary work. I experienced the people of St. Monica's as the Body of Christ in a whole new way. I still run into people who were on that trip with me, and we talk about it. Recounting the experience reminds me to try to be of help to people in whatever way possible. Everybody has a different way he or she can be helpful.

It's a very powerful thing to see people in a situation that is the barest minimum existence. They didn't do anything to deserve that; I didn't do anything to deserve being born into my family. Sure, I've worked hard, and I guess you could say I earned a certain amount of what I have, but am I any different from my Kenyan brothers and sisters in Christ?

No, I don't think so. I try to remind myself that just because I was born on third base doesn't mean I hit a triple. Reflecting on my experience in Kenya calls this truth to mind. I sense, once again, what a very important part of my life my parish has become. It helps me stay grounded; it helps me not lose sight of what's really important; it helps me get out of myself and serve. It got me to Kenya and the transformative experience I had there.

At Parish Catalyst, we say "we are the platform, not the show" and "our fruit grows on others' trees." These are all selfless concepts. Now, I'm not selfless every minute of every day, but I do believe that the more I am in a position to be involved in Parish Catalyst and St. Monica's the more I am of service. The more I'm helping other people the more I am following Christ and the more honest I feel about myself.

7

—

ENTERING THE MISSION FIELD

The Gospel of Jesus Christ is the Power of God and the salvation for all who believe. And as long as I have breath, my mission is to convince everybody I meet that that's true.

—Fr. Jay Scott Newman
St. Mary's, Greenville, South Carolina

Go, therefore, and make disciples of all nations, baptizing them in the name of the Father and of the Son and of the holy Spirit, teaching them to observe all that I have commanded you.

—Matthew 28:19–20, NABRE

There is a church in New Jersey that has a sign over its exit doors that reads "You are now entering your mission field." What a great reminder that reaching out beyond our comfortable faith communities is part and parcel of being Catholic. We are to reach out and share what we have received. Or as the Church would say, we are to evangelize.

Today we need to be even more intentional and creative in living out this charge. One of our pastors put it this way: "We can no longer leave the light on for people; we now have to bring the light to them."

For many of us Catholics, the word *evangelization* evokes one of two responses. Maybe we associate it with overzealous, in-your-face, fire-and-brimstone fanatics, and so we write it off completely. Or we think of it as we think of exercise: we know we should be doing it, but we aren't, so we carry a lot of guilt about not doing it enough or not doing it at all. We feel unfit and unqualified. Jesus' mandate to transform the world by going out and making disciples goes into the "too hard" pile.

Despite its reputation in many Catholic circles as a Protestant phenomenon, evangelization has always been an explicitly stated goal of the Catholic Church. In the document *Go and Make Disciples: A National Plan and Strategy for Catholic Evangelization*,[1] the US Catholic bishops wrote about evangelizing in an inviting and encouraging way: "To bring about in all Catholics such an enthusiasm for their faith that, in living their faith in Jesus, they freely share it with others."[2]

When you think about the times in your life when you have been very enthusiastic—for example, learning to drive, falling in love, landing a job—you realize that sharing your enthusiasm for something is very spontaneous and takes very little effort. At its core, evangelization should be more about passion and joy than it is about a job to do. And you don't even have to be very good at it. As Nobel Prize winner Sir Edward V. Appleton put it, "I rate enthusiasm even above professional skill."[3]

FROM MIRRORS TO WINDOWS, MAINTENANCE TO MISSION

In general, Catholics remain less than enthusiastic about the idea of evangelizing, so it is not surprising that our pastors saw evangelization as an area for growth as often as they mentioned it as a strength in their parishes. Approximately half the pastors we interviewed (49.4 percent) said that their parish is already successfully evangelizing. Other pastors admitted that it is an area of weakness, typically due to a lack of energy and time or the absence of an intentional focus such as a strategic plan, a dedicated staff member, or a working committee. More than half of the pastors (58.6 percent) said that their evangelization efforts need further development. Many of our parishes are only beginning to take the concept of invitation beyond the door of the church to the local neighborhood and to the world at large. That is, they are just beginning to get a handle on evangelization.

EVANGELIZING PEOPLE ARE WINDOW PEOPLE

The mirror people and window people metaphor appears in many places, both religious and secular. "Mirror people" look at the glass and see only themselves. In contrast, "window people" can look through the glass and see others.[4] Evangelizing people are the parishioners who see beyond their parish community and share their enthusiasm for the parish with outsiders, encouraging them to join in. They see the needs of the world and make room in their lives to provide for others.

Fr. Dan Schlegel of Holy Angels parish in Chagrin Falls, Ohio, said:

> I would go back to an editorial that was in *The New York Times* last week that said that we have become mirror people—mirror people who want everyone to look like us, think like us, act like us, vote like us. And the Church has that same danger at times. I think that what the new Holy Father is doing is helping us to become window people, [who] look out the window at a broader world. And if there's any success that I've had here, [it] is that I think that I've helped move people here from being mirror people to being window people who look out at the bigger world.

Fr. Jay Scott Newman of St. Mary's Catholic Church in Greenville, South Carolina, said, "Evangelical Catholicism means I am a Catholic because I believe the Gospel is true. And how any Catholic—including a priest—conceives of being Catholic has practical consequences for the working out of that identity in life."

EVANGELIZING PARISHES ARE MISSION FOCUSED

In order for a parish to become an evangelizing parish, the people who call that parish their spiritual home may need to reframe their understanding of the purpose of a parish. As bestselling author Fr. Richard Rohr, O.F.M., remarked, the parish can no longer be seen purely as a "filling station," whose sole purpose is to fill the needs of its members, but as a "life-saving station," where members grow in maturity of faith and the struggling or seeking stranger can find refuge and answers.[5]

Fr. James Mallon uses the terms *maintenance* and *mission* in his thoughtful and compelling 2014 book *Divine Renovation* to rethink our models of parish life.[6] His book combs through the Church's writings on evangelization and outlines clear and simple ways parishes can take action. *Divine Renovation* has become essential reading for parishes that are ready to move forward in this area.

"Moving from maintenance to mission" is a common way pastors speak about a parish's evolution toward evangelization. "Maintenance parishes" are primarily focused on sustaining their current membership, whereas "mission parishes" are reaching beyond themselves. For Fr. Newman, cultural Catholicism lends itself too easily to what he called "institutional maintenance": "Here is the parish, there is the pastor. We publish the Mass schedule and wait for people to come to us." He contrasted that with evangelical Catholicism, which understands itself to be a missionary enterprise. Evangelical Catholics have marching orders: "go to all nations and teach them everything I have taught you."

Like Fr. Newman, other pastors we heard from have clear visions and strong convictions about what it means to create a culture of evangelization in a parish. The reach beyond the parish touches everything and changes the way the Gospel is lived on the ground.

Fr. Giles LeVasseur, who pastors both St. Mary's and Epiphany parishes in Petersburg, West Virginia, also used these terms to talk about reaching out to grow his parishes: "We're still in 'mission,' meaning we still grow, we're still bringing in new households. . . . We're not just holding on or shrinking like some of the parishes are."

Encouraging evangelization at the parish requires modification of both the culture and the organizational structure of the parish. By culture, we mean the mentality, values, norms, beliefs, and habits the community holds. By structure we mean the framework for how work gets accomplished, how information flows, and how roles and responsibilities are coordinated. In other words:

1. The people of the parish must shift from being mirror people to being window people.

2. The structure of the parish must move from maintenance to mission.

NEW VISION, NEW STRUCTURES

Many of our parishes have adjusted their mindsets in order to become evangelizing parishes. This is not a change in doctrine; it is a change in attitude. It is extraordinarily difficult for a culture of invitation to take root if only a few scattered individuals are willing to move toward a more evangelical outlook. Scale is important, meaning that the whole parish community needs to be on board to keep evangelization afloat.

Changing the culture of any organization is difficult. As Stephen Covey points out in his book *The 7 Habits of Highly Effective People*, you must begin with the end in mind. The "end" that a pastor and staff look for is no less than a community-wide conversion of heart, which is elusive at best. The community needs to become enthusiastic and joyful about their parish and their own relationships with Christ. Without their enthusiasm and joy, a parish cannot sustain an evangelization initiative.

CHANGE STARTS WITH PARISH LEADERSHIP

A culture of invitation does not suddenly appear. It takes a conscious effort on the part of parish leadership. Fr. Jeremy Leatherby of Presentation of the Blessed Virgin Mary parish in Sacramento, California, wants the legacy he eventually leaves his parish to be a culture of evangelization: "Right now, the direction we're headed, something I hope to instill in people—and I've got a team that I'm working with—is to become a parish of evangelization. So often in my entire life, I was this way: as Catholics, you go to church on Sunday and you try to maintain the parish, but there was no sense of 'let's spread the faith to everybody.' If we really believe this, wouldn't we want everybody to be Catholic? And so we're just now becoming a parish that has the mission of evangelizing."

Fr. Tim Fitzgerald of SS. John and Paul parish in Altoona, Iowa, rallied his congregation around one word: *invite*. He explained, "It requires, among other things, a real change in mentality for the pastoral staff, the pastoral leadership. It now requires far closer attention to inviting people and to getting the word out on what's going on. And part of our refrain here, the bite of this challenge, is to keep saying 'invite, invite, invite.' That's a big factor with the staff energy here and communications here and starting things here."

As Fr. Fitzgerald expressed, culture change begins with the leadership team. Many parishes begin by focusing staff goals and parish meetings on the creation of a spirit of invitation. Once the staff is on board, some parishes form an evangelization committee to initiate this new invitational culture. One rural parish we spoke with focused on the spiritual and professional development of staff explicitly to ensure that a culture of invitation was understood and accepted by leadership. A suburban parish set administrative and organizational topics aside for a period of time to allow for a more focused development of evangelization. Both of these parishes provided a time for staff to concentrate on the parish's new initiative before launching it in the parish.

INVOLVING THE WHOLE PARISH

Even if the culture of the parish is to "invite, invite, invite," this is more actionable if parishioners know how to put it into practice. Parish evangelization campaigns and initiatives provide staff members with a clear sense of responsibility and a clear understanding of the work that needs to be done. At the same time, the campaigns and initiatives give parishioners the information and opportunities they need in order to understand and participate in the new parish vision.

Msgr. Charles Pope of Holy Comforter-St. Cyprian Church in Washington, DC, saw great success in his parish's evangelization efforts over the previous six years in large part because of structured reaching: "Everybody gets involved. I had forty people knocking on doors while forty more were praying in the chapel for our success. And another forty were signed up to provide a meal for the prayers and the walkers when they got back. So, on a typical Saturday morning during evangelization season, we've got 120 people. It isn't just some little subcommittee of niche people who were willing to get out and knock on a few doors. It's a fairly big cross-section of the parish that are involved." Giving people jobs and a structure to work with—knocking on doors, praying, providing meals, and so on—makes evangelization less vague and more actionable.

Getting the word out that new people belong at the parish is easier when there is a structured plan. One parish we spoke with in Missouri uses a scatter diagram to keep track of where parishioners live. The parish hosts picnics at local parks, inviting neighbors and those who live down the street. Once an initial contact is established, it is only a matter of consulting the diagram to see which parishioner lives nearby and can follow up with someone who has already made that first step toward the parish.

Some parishes we spoke with were having success using established evangelization programs. Others spoke highly of books on the subject that have been very helpful. Programs and resources these pastors mentioned include Bishop Robert Barron's *Catholicism* series, Alpha in a Catholic Context (and Alpha Plus), Kenneth C. Haugk's *Caring for Inactive Members: How to Make God's House a Home*, the seven-week Discovering Christ program, and Sherry Weddell's *Forming Intentional Disciples*.

Developing enthusiasm for evangelization in parishioners can be a slow process. Fr. Erik Arnold of Our Lady of Perpetual Help parish in Ellicott City, Maryland, understands what a paradigm shift it can be for parishioners to turn their faith and religion more outward. When asked if the courses mentioned above helped people share their faith, he acknowledged, "It's the area where I think our parishioners are most challenged." He perceived the need for baby steps, beginning with inviting people whom parishioners already know and trust (a family member or a friend). "They are not ready to say, 'Jesus loves you! Come check it out,'" said Fr. Arnold. So he suggests something more low-key: "Look, we've got this going on at the parish, and I really think you'd like it. And, if you'd like, I'll go each week with you."

OPENING DOORS

In the end, the purpose of evangelization is not to "make converts" or "fill the pews" but simply to open doors—to let others know the Good News that Catholic faith has made a positive difference in our lives and that God's love is available to others as well. Evangelizing parishes disciple parishioners by developing small groups and other opportunities that teach parishioners about their faith and how to be more at ease sharing it. They also create programs of welcome and parish strategies with an outward focus that intentionally provide an easy entrée for people who are searching. Evangelizing opportunities include community-service programs, social events, sacramental celebrations, and mission work.

COMMUNITY-SERVICE PROGRAMS

Many Catholic churches run highly successful community-service programs. But the pastors we spoke with expressed an interest in moving from simple charity to something deeper, focusing on the spiritual motivation that underlies the community service. For example, parishioners can encourage individuals who come to a meal program or food pantry to join the parish. Parishioners are not there merely to serve people but also to invite them to become part of the community if they do not already have a church home.

Fr. Michael Woods of All Saints parish in Knoxville, Tennessee, explained his approach to community-service organizations using an example many Catholics are familiar with: "I'm not big for organizations just for organizations' sake. It has to be an outreach. I know it's an ancient thing, but we just set up a Knights of Columbus group because they've been bugging me for years. We did, and more than a hundred men came into it, and not just to socialize. You have to reach out with the Gospel and find a way to serve. I feel that's what our parish is."

SOCIAL EVENTS

Several pastors talked about developing social occasions that had no overt "join our church" hook. Such secular activities forge initial contact with new people. Friendship and familiarity can pave the way for a future invitation to worship.

One of the challenges is to offer high-quality events that intersect with the personal interests of a large enough number of unchurched people to justify the effort and the related costs. The competition is not other church events but all the public offerings available in the entertainment and business world. A well-planned and -executed event is a "safe" way for the churchless to be introduced to the people, environment, and culture of the church. According to the Barna Group, the two most effective ways to be positioned in the minds of the unchurched[7] are

- as a ministry that regularly and effectively serves the needs of the poor, and

- as a church that understands young people and provides the kind of mentoring and development they need to thrive in life.[8]

Events that fulfill one or both of these parameters work to further evangelizing efforts while still serving the parish mission.

SACRAMENTAL MOMENTS

Along similar lines, some pastors see weddings, funerals, and baptisms as important opportunities for connecting with people who are unchurched. These are significant life events when people who do not attend church will come to support their friends and family. Msgr. Pope of Holy Comforter-St. Cyprian parish in Washington, DC, spoke emphatically about the evangelization opportunity at one of these moments:

> We mess up with funerals because 80 percent of the
> people in a typical funeral are unchurched. Most of

them are not praying. They are not serious about their spiritual life. They're just there because Joe died. And many of them are in very serious, unrepented mortal sin. And they need to hear from me. So, with a little bit of humor, but also a little bit of an emphatic call, I say, "Get right with God. You're going to die. Joe's your teacher today. And by God, you're going to die; what are you doing to get ready to meet God? Now listen, I'm saying to you in the name of Jesus [that] nobody loves you more than Jesus. Turn to him. Start praying, read scripture. Get to church on Sunday."

GLOBAL MISSIONS

Reaching out globally through mission work is another aspect of evangelization that is increasingly popular. Mission work was mentioned by one-third of our pastors. A great source of genuine hope for the Catholic Church right now lies in this movement toward a radical hospitality that reaches beyond parishes and into homes and lives around the globe. Pastors described to us successful missions in a variety of locations around the world, including Honduras, Haiti, Nicaragua, Kenya, El Salvador, Dominican Republic, Peru, Jamaica, Guatemala, Appalachia, New Jersey (after Hurricane Sandy), and Louisiana and Mississippi (after Hurricane Katrina).

One pastor's enthusiasm and joy for not only the missions themselves but also the benefits they can bestow on the missionaries fueled a sense of excitement for missionary work in his parish. Fr. Matt Foley of St. James Church in Arlington Heights, Illinois, insisted that he is "aggressive in evangelization." For many years, his parish reached out locally to young people, inviting them to ministries such as youth choirs. They entered people's homes and invited them into the sanctuary. They connected individuals to a personal relationship with Jesus.

Then they decided to do the same thing in Mexico. For six years they practiced door-to-door evangelization, led Bible studies, and helped people forge a connection with the Eucharist. Fr. Foley saw that the mission work created and deepened discipleship in his people: "You really learn a lot more about your faith by teaching it than by saying you're inadequate because we're all inadequate. The apostles felt inadequate. But Jesus told the apostles, 'I am the Way, the Truth, and the Life.' And he'll help you when you go out in your two-by-two missions. So I think that's always been a reason we've been successful. We don't wait for people to come; we go out and find them. You have to go outside the temple precincts." Fr. Foley's assertiveness infused his parish with an evangelical spirit in which national and regional borders take a back seat to spreading the Good News; this creates new disciples while also deepening discipleship in the missionaries.

For a pastor in a Northeast suburb, missions are about going out into the world to discover what God wants you to do. This rings true in his parish, where the evangelization program grew steadily over the last decade as people signed up for missions to New Orleans, Nicaragua, Africa, and Appalachia.

THE FRANCIS EFFECT

Throughout our interviews, pastors brought up Pope Francis as a model for evangelization and outreach, a figure with not only the capacity to energize active Catholics but also the ability to inspire the broader ecumenical and secular world. Said Fr. Daniel Andrews of Sacred Heart parish in Norfolk, Nebraska, "I see our greatest opportunity as reaching out and meeting those who are inactive—that is, if we are willing to stop looking inside at ourselves and look out and make our church a welcoming place."

The Holy Father came up in 33 percent of our interviews, despite not being part of our protocol of questions. That's an amazing statistic! Pope Francis is a key figure in modeling evangelization as a way of life on a global scale. Fr. Frederick Pausche of St. Gabriel Church in Concord Township, Ohio, remarked, "We're trying to strengthen that whole idea of service as a way of life and trying to respond to the Holy Father's call to go beyond ourselves—not just do things within our parish boundaries and on our property and for our good, but rather, get out there into the wider community and bring the Gospel out there."

Pope Francis has encouraged dialogue about issues that have long been difficult to raise in the Catholic Church. His openness to conversations about tough topics offers many Catholics a route to freedom from shame in the wake of scandals from which we are still healing. Moreover, Pope Francis is nourishing spiritual hunger, such that distinct variations of the "Francis effect" are manifest among clergy, the Catholic community, and the broader public. His paradigm shift—from receiving new disciples to pursuing them—resonates in a time when parish affiliation and Mass attendance cannot be taken for granted even in historic strongholds of Catholicism.

Our pastors described people "making steps back to the Church" or "making inquiries into the life of the Church." Fr. Ron Lewinski of St. Mary of the Annunciation in Mundelein, Illinois, commented, "I just came back from Vienna, [where] my great-nephew works for the State Department. He doesn't consider himself a Catholic anymore. He's twenty-nine. I don't know that he ever was really into it. But he was asking me about Pope Francis, and he said that his peers in the State Department, young people like himself, have been fascinated by Francis, and in his words, they're taking a second look at the Catholic Church."

Fr. Mark Horak of Holy Trinity parish in Washington, DC, described the pope's effect as one of "capturing people's imagination." He said, "I think Pope Francis seems to have energized people and drawn people's attention back to the larger Church, and that, I think, is a real opportunity. In fact, even just today, in reaction to the interview that Francis gave a couple days ago, I've gotten lots of email comments from parishioners, even a couple of phone calls from people who haven't been to church for a while, believe it or not, and they seem—they seem excited about being Catholic."

Fr. J. Mark Hobson of Church of the Resurrection in Solon, Ohio, concurred: "It seems like this is an opportunity to focus on what we can unite around, and to stop battling [over] what we disagree about.

People have been so much more positive about the Church around here since he was elected."

CRUCIAL TAKEAWAYS

1. The pastors we interviewed saw evangelization as an area needing growth (58.6 percent) a little more often than they mentioned it as a strength (49.9 percent).

2. The whole parish community needs to be on board in order to create and sustain an evangelizing culture. Individuals need to become window people (p. 140–143), and parishes need to become mission focused.

3. Evangelizing parishes intentionally create an attractive culture of invitation and structured reaching using service programs, social events, celebration of the sacraments, and missions work.

4. The leadership witness of Pope Francis is opening new avenues for parish-level evangelization.

8

—

CHALLENGES TO EVANGELIZATION

Our biggest opportunity is to reach out and engage those who are inactive. It dooms us if we don't do that. So I think that's every parish's opportunity: . . . not just to be somewhat happy that people come in your doors. Catholics need to turn that corner of taking an interest and putting yourself out on a limb for other people. We have to do that.

—Fr. Dan Andrews
Sacred Heart, Norfolk, Nebraska

RELUCTANCE TO EVANGELIZE

Catholics are known for many things, such as our devotion to the Blessed Mother, ashes on our foreheads on Ash Wednesday, and our understanding of the Real Presence in the Eucharist. One thing that generally does not come to mind when you hear the word *Catholic* is evangelization. This is perhaps why 26.8 percent of our pastors consider evangelization a major challenge.

Through the years Catholics have traditionally viewed their relationship with God as a highly personal matter and believed that overt evangelizing comes dangerously close to imposing one's religious beliefs on others. Although, as seen in the chapter 7, new strategies at the parish level may produce more evangelical Catholics in the future, Catholics today remain less likely than other Christians to evangelize.[1]

HESITANT INDIVIDUALS

In the previous chapter we talked about the need for Catholics to develop a mindset about their faith that would encourage them to freely share it. It is helpful to look at the reasons behind the "holy hesitancy" that many American Catholics have regarding evangelization. This hesitancy has roots as far back as the colonial era but also owes something to the fast-paced changes that have taken place in secular culture since the 1960s.

Anti-Catholic sentiment has existed in this country since colonial days. In 1642, the Colony of Virginia enacted a law barring Catholic settlers. Five years later, the Massachusetts Bay Colony enacted a similar statute. In the second half of the nineteenth century, nativists and others opposed to immigration (which at the time consisted mostly of Catholics) saw Catholics as papists whose first allegiance would always be to Rome and who therefore could never be truly full-fledged citizens of the republic.

Catholics kept their heads down, lived together in close communities, built their own schools, and married other Catholics. Understandably, about the last thing they expected to do was evangelize. They might assemble to hear a great Catholic orator such as Isaac Hecker,[2] but religion was for the most part a private matter. By the end of the nineteenth century there were nearly thirty different nationality subgroups in the United States that were predominantly Catholic. These subgroups were neither ethnically nor linguistically similar.[3] Even if they had wanted to explain their faith to someone, most would not have had the words for it.

Fast-forward to the 1960s, which ushered in a rapid change in the secular culture. Catholics became fully assimilated into American life. For the first time, a Catholic was indistinguishable from anyone else in society. Simultaneously the universal Church experienced the Second Vatican Council, which changed a great deal of Catholic institutional and religious self-understanding.[4] For the first time, Catholics were encouraged to interact fully with people of other faiths.[5] This worldview ushered in a form of cultural Catholicism that is "'comfortable' because it fit[s] neatly within the ambient public culture, causing little chafing between one's life 'in the Church' and one's life 'in the world.'"[6] Though socially accepted and assimilated, Catholics continued to keep faith a private matter; they finally fit in, which became a new reason to keep their faith to themselves.

INSULAR COMMUNITIES

Parish life is busy. It is easy for a parish's leadership to work hard and yet, over time, see their parish become an insular, comfortable place where current parishioners come to pray, receive sacraments, do some outreach to the poor, and have their children participate in school or parish activities. One Virginian pastor talked about this:

> They could become basically complacent and not go out of their way to invite their neighbors or not go out of their way to mention it to their coworkers. And so a lot of people could have a bunker mentality where "I go to church because I need to get my needs filled." So my struggle has to do with that opportunity. There are a lot of people who need God. There are many more people that need prayer, that need grace, that need the sacraments. And sometimes when you get beleaguered, you convince yourself that nobody else is interested in what we're doing; it's just us, just our small little group. And instead they need to be encouraged that this really is attractive to a lot of people. You just have to reach out to them.

Some pastors struggled with their parish leadership's inability to focus on anything that does not directly affect the parish. A pastor from the South described a faction of his parishioners who focused primarily on building a new gym and providing parishioners with various services. Another southern pastor expressed the overarching issue plainly: "One of the things I think the Catholic Church was very guilty of was spending a lot more time saving the saved than reaching out to those beyond."

An Illinois pastor believes the leadership inside his parish looks at the challenge of reaching people the wrong way: "Inevitably what happens, I'm finding, is that they can't think beyond themselves. So they may come up with an idea for how to revitalize the parish, an idea such as, hypothetically here, we need to say the Rosary after every Mass in our parish. Well, that's very nice, except that the people next door to me are not so sure they even believe in God at this point. So whom are you doing this for?"

This pastor did not let his congregation shoulder all the blame; he also lamented his own struggles with reaching people:

> Many people have given up on the Church and figure, "Well, the Church isn't going to help me with the questions I have." How can we break that cycle? It's like a glass ceiling; it's so hard to break through the barrier out there that we're not breaking through somehow. It's like, "Give me a chance! Sit down with me for a little bit and talk about that. Then I could talk you into something that you haven't thought about before." How do I have that conversation with that person? How do I find that person? I find that very problematic: how to reach beyond our borders.

ATTRITION

According to the Pew Research Center, between 2007 and 2014, the Christian share of the US population fell from 78.4 percent to 70.6 percent, driven mainly by declines among mainline Protestants and Catholics. The Catholic share alone dropped from 23.9 percent to 20.8 percent. Americans who belong to non-Christian faiths increased, but the unaffiliated experienced the most growth.[7]

As the ranks of the religiously unaffiliated continue to grow, they also describe themselves in increasingly secular terms. The atheist and agnostic share of the religiously unaffiliated reached to 31 percent in 2014, while those identifying as "nothing in particular" and describing religion as unimportant in their lives accounted for 39 percent of the unaffiliated.

According to the Pew report, "Within Christianity the greatest net losses, by far, have been experienced by Catholics. Nearly one-third of American adults (31.7%) say they were raised Catholic. Among that group, fully 41% no longer identify with Catholicism. This means that 12.9% of American adults are former Catholics, while just 2% of American adults have converted to Catholicism from another religious tradition. No other religious group in the Pew survey has such a lopsided ratio of losses to gains."[8] Figure 8.1 compares this trend with those for Protestant churches and for the ranks of the unaffiliated.

Some of the losses in the Catholic Church are to other Christian denominations. The deep divide that once existed between Protestants and Catholics, which made religious switching almost unheard of in previous times, is no longer a deterrent for many Catholics. As a personal example, my five sisters were all raised Catholic. Four now attend churches of other Christian denominations. Only one still attends a Catholic church.

Many pastors (54.8 percent) brought up concerns related to attrition, inactive and lapsed Catholics, and those that are being called the "unchurched" and the "nones." They expressed deep concern and sorrow over the lack of progress they saw around the pressing need for evangelization. Some said they felt "sad and regretful" and voiced concern that "the Catholic Church has lost both focus and the ability to bring people to experience the power of Jesus in their lives."

Although discouraged, the pastors clearly have a desire to rise to the challenge. They are committed to welcoming the unaffiliated, inviting the neighbor, and finding the Catholics we have lost; they seek to "bring people back to the message of the Gospel" and "evangelize the inactives."

Msgr. Michael Henchal of St. John and Holy Cross parish in South Portland, Maine, remarked, "How do we reach out to those folks that have really disappeared from any form of church life at all, whether former Catholics or those of other backgrounds?" An answer to that

Figure 8.1 Unaffiliated on the rise

FROM 2007 TO 2014

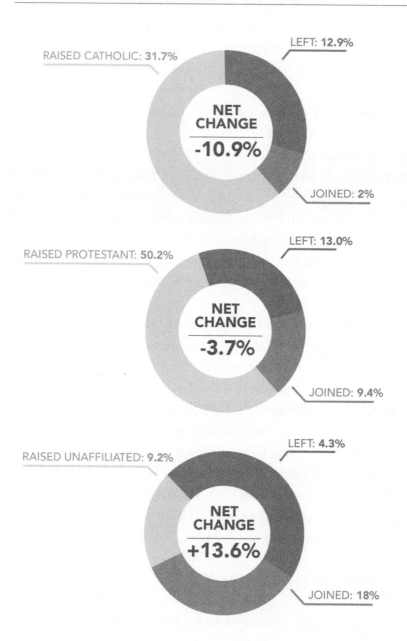

RAISED CATHOLIC: **31.7%**

LEFT: **12.9%**

NET CHANGE
-10.9%

JOINED: **2%**

RAISED PROTESTANT: **50.2%**

LEFT: **13.0%**

NET CHANGE
-3.7%

JOINED: **9.4%**

RAISED UNAFFILIATED: **9.2%**

LEFT: **4.3%**

NET CHANGE
+13.6%

JOINED: **18%**

PEW RESEARCH CENTER, MAY 2015

question might come in the form of a question asked by Msgr. Drake Shafer of St. Ann's parish in Long Grove, Iowa: "How can we be inclusive, welcoming, forgiving, and healing?"

REACHING MILLENNIALS

A large proportion of our pastors (33.9 percent) reflected concern for reaching the millennial generation specifically. The Pew study mentioned above found that, in 2014, more than one-third of adults in the millennial generation (35 percent) said they had no religion, up 10 points from 2007. One of our pastors called millennial ministry the "most significant challenge" faced by the Church today.

Those born anywhere between the early 1980s and the early 2000s are often categorized as millennials.[9] In 2015, the millennial generation became the largest living generation in the United States, eclipsing generation X and the baby boomers. The generation continues to grow as young immigrants expand its ranks. As millennials number more than 75 million,[10] it is no surprise that everyone from advertisers to politicians is clamoring to figure this generation out and discover how to appeal to them.

A DIFFERENT BREED

It is well known that millennials are the Internet generation. They read less and watch more, which makes them a visual-learning generation.[11] Most have spent the majority of their lives with instant access to people and information. The window to their world, generally speaking, is a screen, and much of the information they process is delivered in small, digestible packets.

Fr. Joe Fortuna of Our Lady of the Lake parish in Euclid, Ohio, shared insights he gained regarding the way millennials think and process when he taught an online course. "One of the things I discovered," he said, "is I'm not a digital native. My thinking tends to be linear. That's different from a digital native who thinks in hyperlink fashion. [Digital natives] read an article or get partway through an article, and they see something and click on it. They get partway through that, and they click again—and they are perfectly comfortable with that. To the degree that this shapes how people think, it ought to shape how we consider talking with them, reaching out to them."

Recent changes to higher American education have also had a significant impact on the millennials' life experience. In their book *Spiritual Formation in Emerging Adulthood*, David Setran and Chris Kiesling point out that the "expansion and extension" of higher education, coupled with its rising costs, have delayed significant adult milestones.[12] Sociologists mark five key events as material to entering adulthood: leaving home, finishing school, establishing financial independence, getting married, and having children. In 1960, more than two-thirds of young adults attained all five of these markers by age thirty. By 2000, this was true of fewer than half of the women and fewer than a third of the men.[13]

A 2013 study by the American Psychological Association found that millennials experience greater anxiety than older generations.[14] More millennials have been diagnosed with depression and anxiety disorders than previous generations.[15] Many have no idea what they will be doing, where they will be living, or who they will be within two or even ten years.

There is certainly a need for faith in these young lives, but as Fr. Martin Linebach of St. Patrick Church in Louisville, Kentucky, put it, "There's an appetite, but we don't have the menu yet." Fr. Patrick Mullen of Padre Serra parish in Camarillo, California, acknowledged,"My sense is [that] younger people are coming to church and *not* experiencing Jesus, for whatever reason. Whatever it is that we're doing, we're not setting that [encounter] up for them. There's something that we are doing that does not touch the mind, the heart, the life experience of the [millennial]."

Muhammad Yunus once said, "My greatest challenge has been to change the mindset of people. Mindsets play strange tricks on us. We see things the way our minds have instructed our eyes to see."[16] Churches, like businesses and even parents, will need a change of mindset in order to understand and communicate with our young people. Following the recipe from the past is simply not working.

Parishes require new, creative approaches if they are going to be successful with the millennial generation. Fr. Stephen Banet of St. Jude parish in Indianapolis expressed this well: "We need more creative evangelization. We do have a great parish, but that young adult—from college age to the [age when the] first child [is] entering into school—that's an area for young families, young adults, young singles, where we need to work on more creative evangelization, to keep them connected with the parish, and how they can be disciples at this time. . . . How do we keep them engaged and involved?"

NO SURE RETURN

The majority of our pastors who view reaching the millennial generation as a challenge are at least one generation older than the generation they are hoping to reach. They remember a time when estrangement from the Church was considered a product of youthful experimentation. There was every expectation that as young people matured, married, and had families they would rejoin the Church. Certainly, there are studies that show that a contingent of those who leave the Church as young adults do rejoin it either at marriage or the birth of a child.[17] One pastor exemplified this mindset, figuring the lack of participation by the twenty-somethings in his parish was because they are currently in a dynamic time in their lives when they are raising families, attending school, or in the armed services.

However, it appears increasingly likely that many millennials will not return once they have left and that the process of leaving and returning was less a product of developmental patterns than it was distinctive of a particular generation—the baby boomers. According to the Barna Group, the boomers (born 1946 to 1964) were the first American generation to drop out of church participation in significant numbers when they reached young adulthood.[18] Prior to the boomers, evidence suggests, young adults were *not* less churched than their older adult counterparts.[19] According to the Barna Group, "Young people are dropping out earlier, staying away longer, and if they come back are less likely to see the church as a long-term part of their life."[20] To put it differently, because today's young adults continue the trend begun by the boomers, it is becoming a more complex problem with potentially greater consequences for the Church.

MAKING CHURCH WORK

For Fr. Donald Snyder of St. Ladislas parish in Westlake, Ohio, the young adults to target are those already on the periphery of the parish: "I think the challenge is to reach out to those who are not engaged and who are on the fringes of the Church. They call themselves Catholic, but they're just out there." Barna's David Kinnaman refers to these young adults as "nomads." Indeed, they are "around," attending Mass a couple of times a year in many cases, but still have fundamentally disengaged from a Christian identity.[21]

Those young adults who do have an interest in practicing their faith criticize the Christian churches for making so little effort to be relevant to their daily lives. They want to be Christian without separating themselves from the world around them.[22] Thirty-nine percent say they can "find God elsewhere," and twenty percent say "it feels like God is missing from Church."[23]

A parish rarely has a single, monolithic group of young adults, and each community will have its own needs to discern. Fr. Ken Simpson of St. Clement Church in Chicago identified two primary groups of young adults in his parish: young families and college-aged young adults. Of the former, he said, "I don't think this parish has seen itself as a family parish, and it isn't strictly a family parish, but . . . there are a lot more kids around [now]. Parents are asking for our help in raising their kids in the faith. It's a great opportunity to listen, first of all, to what parents are asking for." Of the latter group, young adults still in college or of that age, he said, "It's a very strong group, but their sense of the Church is probably a little more traditional than mine, and so it's an opportunity and a challenge to really listen to that, speak to that, minister in ways that they will help us identify."

Several pastors started by working on a specific problem. For example, Fr. Steve Orr of Our Lady's Immaculate Heart parish in Ankeny, Iowa, observed that many of the single young adults in his parish did not like "to come to church by themselves." In response, he and the rest of his ministry staff made a conscious effort to help these young adults "feel a part of the larger community." Once there was cohesion in the young adult ministry, he reasoned, these young people would feel as though they had come to church together.

Fr. William Thaden of Sacred Heart Chapel in Lorain, Ohio, noticed that his community had a large number of young Mexican families, but parents were not often bringing their children to Mass. The parish leadership asked some questions: "How can we as a parish be more welcoming and supportive to families raising children? Do we have facilities for that kind of thing? We've got to be more family-friendly and kid-friendly. There is a huge energy in an immigrant population, and the church community can become a very important anchor for them."

Nativity of the Blessed Virgin Mary Cathedral in Biloxi, Mississippi, is situated near a military training facility with an influx of young airmen and their families. "Our attention, our focus, is on that air force base," said their pastor, Fr. Dennis Carver. When the staff judged that the distance between the base and the parish school was a problem for some families, they began to work on a bus service.

For other parishes, other types of affinity groups have had traction among young families. For one pastor, a "young couples" group was the ticket—and has now grown to fifty couples. Blessed Sacrament parish in Wichita, Kansas, uses a Cana Couples' group for couples who've been married fewer than fifteen years, and the pastor, Fr. John Jirak, cited renewed energy and increased participation in the parish as a direct result: "There needs to be some kind of social community unit among other couples their age . . . just a fun night, and things keep emerging out of that." Fr. Jirak noted another feature of all their young adult programming, something that allows young families to participate: babysitting is provided for everything.

While some pastors described their millennial population as stereotypical "bleeding hearts," other pastors work with a more traditional millennial population. These young adults are less interested in outreach and social justice than they are in private devotions. They have less interest in serving at the soup kitchen than in praying the Rosary. For Fr. Carl Schlichte, O.P., of St. Catherine of Siena Newman Center in Salt Lake City, Utah, "the first concern of [our] millennials is not service, though they have a great heart for service. They're much more interested in the prayer life, the liturgy, and those types of areas. They tend to go more traditional, more what John Paul II was doing, [though] this is painting in really broad strokes."

Fr. Moe Larochelle of Ste. Marie parish in Manchester, New Hampshire, reported that "the parish has attracted younger people who have a taste for something more traditional. And it's been interesting. . . . You have the formality of younger families who are coming in suit and tie every week, no matter how hot it is."

This kind of discernment-based strategizing allows parishes to be culturally sensitive to the local young adults they serve, inviting them to participate in a ministry that not only has been tailored for their spiritual growth but also takes into consideration what else must exist (e.g., bus service, babysitting) to make it possible for them to participate.

Ultimately, rather than seeing young people as a resource to tap or a market to appeal to, the parishes we spoke with that are successfully engaging young adults are making connections in three distinct ways. As figure 8.2 shows, they connect with millennials through dialogue, mentorship, and leadership opportunities.

HONEST DIALOGUE

A healthy space for dialogue is free from assumptions about young adults. Generalizations about millennials and their preferences can be misleading, and many pastors are finding that the millennials in their midst are not what they expected.

When you ask millennials why they walked away from organized Christianity, you will most likely find them responding that the Church is judgmental, full of hypocrites, too political, too exclusive, elitist, or old-fashioned.[24] Their perspectives may come from a wound they received in the past or from a jaded perspective about formalized religion.

Figure 8.2 Connecting with millennials

LISTEN TO QUESTIONS.
HAVE AUTHENTIC DIALOGUE.

PROVIDE
A MENTOR.

LET THEM LEAD
EACH OTHER.

This generation wants to talk with people they see as real and transparent. They want the freedom to doubt and to ask hard questions. Some of our pastors understood the first step to evangelizing millennials as welcoming these questions. For Msgr. Charles Pope at Holy Comforter-St. Cyprian parish in Washington, DC, traction came when Theology on Tap, a lecture program that addresses current topics in religion and theology in a bar or restaurant, inspired him to develop less structured talks. He said,

> What I want to start is what I call "Grill the Pastor" or "Grill the Priest," where we have [a] smaller, more intimate setting, where maybe the priest will give a ten-minute talk, just to introduce some [ideas], get

people thinking—but then people ask anything they want, just grill the priest. People have a lot of questions, and they have struggles, so what I want to try to do is, in certain settings with young adults especially, say, "Well, what are your strengths, what are your struggles, what are your hopes, your joys? Talk to me, and I'll be happy to [answer] questions. What do you want to hear? What do you wonder about?"

Fr. Brian Lang of St. Charles and St. Ann parish in Syracuse, New York, has been trying a similar program he calls BYOF—"Bring Your Own Faith." The initiative is intended to give young adults "an opportunity . . . to come and talk about particular issues in the Church they have problems with."

At Parish of the Precious Blood in Caribou, Maine, the young adults, for the most part, came from families with no church involvement and were intentionally looking for something different for themselves. Their pastor, Fr. Jean-Paul Labrie, said, "They're coming in [knowing] they don't want to live with what their parents lived [with], and they're looking for what was not given to them [by their parents], and they're very open, not at all critical about teachings or the position that the Catholic Church takes. They're very sincere about getting a structure in their life that's going to help them be a good person . . . and I'm intrigued by that."

For all of these pastors, an understanding of who these young adults are emerged from authentic conversation, free of preconceived notions of who they might be.

MENTORING RELATIONSHIPS

Everyone wants to know someone "farther down the trail" who believes in them, whether it's through mentorship, coaching, guiding, discipling, or training. But millennials are particularly open to trusted mentorship.[25]

Millennials who remained in a Christian church beyond their teen years are twice as likely to have a close personal friendship with an older adult in their faith as those who have left.[26] The Church is one of the final remaining intergenerational spaces in modern American society. While affinity groups designed to attract and connect young adults of a similar age or experience do well in many communities, the opportunity for connection to people of other ages and experiences is valued by this generation. Fr. Carl Schlichte, O.P., pastor of St. Catherine of Siena Newman Center in Salt Lake City, Utah, remarked that one of his parish's greatest strengths is that they are "intentionally multigenerational."

Fr. Brian Lang of St. Charles and St. Ann parish in Syracuse, New York, shared an interesting aspect of parish life:

> To be able to [do ministry], you have to [take into consideration] the multigenerational experience that each parish has today in terms of the pre–Vatican II people and the Vatican II people, the post–Vatican II people, the gen X people, the gen Y people, now millennials. You have to be able to at least make a valid attempt to invite each of those groups into an experience individually, so that they have their own experience that they can share with their contemporary group, and then you can bring them together. If you can make those connections between younger and other generations, it helps an enormous amount, building up the churches.

Whether or not a pastor is able to engage a young adult in his community directly, he can intentionally enable cross-generational sharing that allows for authentic mentorship. The best resource for modeling for young adults how to live as Christians in the "real world" may be older Christians in the pews who have done it for some time. A starting place for this sort of mentorship can be an all-church event. Fr. John DiBacco of St. Mary's parish in Morgantown, West Virginia, remarked, "We get college students at those [faith formation] events, and we get senior citizens. We get middle-aged people and all that. And they just come—there's no cost—they come and they begin to meet friends because they'll start sitting at tables together. You can see that develop over the years we've been doing it." These events, interestingly, were designed for young adults but drew a much broader, multigenerational audience.

Mentorship need not observe geographical boundaries. Even though the young adults affiliated with a parish may not be physically present, it is still possible to include them in parish ministry. A member of one parish decided she wanted to do something for the college kids who were going away, "so she began to send out just a little 'We're thinking of you' kind of thing and, at Christmas and finals, 'We're praying for you' and . . . some kind of candy bar. She's getting a great response. . . . [Parents] say that the kids like to get the cards."

Msgr. Thomas Mullin of St. Elizabeth Ann Seton parish in Uwchlan, Pennsylvania, commented that "because we have so many young people and they are looking for some meaning and purpose beyond the everydayness of things . . . the harvest is ripe." Research stemming from our study indicates that mentorship is most relevant if spiritual guidance is substantively linked to the other aspects of a young person's life. A mentor who gives identical or formulaic advice has not first dialogued with the young person and will be less effective than a mentor whose advice is applicable and germane to the individual's circumstance.

Mentoring is not necessarily a one-on-one process. Some of our pastors looked at the needs of a segment of their millennial population and provided opportunities with them in mind. Msgr. Doug Cook of Holy Family parish in Orange, California, saw the needs of young families in his parish and began a program in which parents and children were mentored through spiritual growth opportunities at a time when parents could also meet their Sunday obligation. "We've recently started a very exciting program called Faith and Family Nights, which had [more than] two hundred people show up, with young families, on Saturday night. Faith, nourishment, and then a simple little Vigil Mass. . . . [We] bring in a speaker for the young adults and some faith projects for the kids in various groups."

Cambria Tortorelli, parish life director at Holy Family parish in South Pasadena, California, recognized a mentoring opportunity and plans to provide parenting classes. The parish wants to emulate a local Presbyterian church renowned for its parenting classes, which were so widely attended that even young families from the parish were paying hundreds of dollars to attend. She said, "We've been talking about emulating and [even] improving on a wonderful model of parenting classes that are offered . . . [so young families] can attend these several-week courses for different ages of children. We need to do something like that here and embed in that some spiritual growth and guidance and support for these young families that are really stretched in so many different ways."

LEADERSHIP OPPORTUNITIES

The parishes whose young adult ministries experienced the greatest success created opportunities for young adults to lead.

Fr. Adan Sandoval of Our Lady of the Mount in Cicero, Illinois, said, "As a staff here [we have] a bunch of young people who have a tremendous love for the Church, and that makes a huge difference." Fr. Tom Lily of St. Elizabeth Ann Seton parish in Anchorage, Alaska, said of one of his staff members: "I would literally match our young adult and youth minister up against anyone in the whole United States. I don't mean that in a triumphal way. . . . The Lord really blessed us with an outstanding youth and young adult minister. It took two years of praying and waiting and searching and interviewing." Another pastor received a grant to send ten of his parish leaders to Loyola Institute of Ministry for a master's degree in pastoral studies and planned to choose mostly "younger folks."

Young adults are particularly well equipped for leadership roles when it comes to inviting other young adults. Fr. Bob Campbell of Our Lady of the Most Holy Rosary parish in Albuquerque, New Mexico, remarked that their youth evangelize other youth. "The greatest success of the parish, I would say, is our youth and young adult program. Our youth and young adult team, which are basically youth and young adults themselves, go to other parishes, to train them how to set up youth and young adult programs in their parishes." Fr. Paul Manning of St. Paul Inside the Walls parish in Madison, New Jersey, remarked that "one of our very intentional outreaches here is to the young adult community, and we do have an active young adult community, run by young adults—young adults ministering to other young adults."

Fr. Gary Lazzeroni of St. Joseph parish in Vancouver, Washington, cited his young parochial vicar as a great resource in gathering young adult couples. Fr. Lazzeroni said, "He was a young guy, so it was kind of natural for him. The young folks were attracted to him and his style, so one of the things I asked him to do—because we knew he wasn't going to be here forever—was to really enable leadership within that group, so that when he left, [others] would take it on. They have, in ways beyond my wildest dreams. It's very exciting that we have this very vibrant group of young adults."

Young people want to identify themselves with social roles that give them a sense of belonging and purpose. When ministry offerings are designed with this desire in mind, they are more likely to be successful. Fr. Brian Lang of St. Charles and St. Ann parish in Syracuse, New York, said, "We made a commitment in the last month to our young people to get them involved in NCYC [National Catholic Youth Conference] and to open up experiences for them in leadership in the church, and I think that's our greatest opportunity now."

Fr. Matt Foley at St. James parish in Arlington Heights, Illinois, which has six Masses on a given weekend, has devoted a Mass to young adults and high-school youth in order to "make a more considered effort [to reach] out to our young people." Fr. Ben Hawley, S.J., of St. Mary Student Parish in Ann Arbor, Michigan, solicited undergraduate parishioners to teach CCD or religious education to parish children: "The parents love this because their children won't necessarily listen to other adults but the kids love the idea that they've got college students teaching them. We always have sixty or seventy undergraduates in these programs."

TECH AND THE GOSPEL

We are meant to speak the Gospel in the language of today; that language is technology, and millennials aren't the only ones immersed in it. Technology is today's *lingua franca,* and our pastors see it as "a resource that we can use for God's glory."[27]

This said, many realize they have a long way to go to make full use of technology. When asked what keeps him up at night, Msgr. Doug Cook of Holy Family parish in Orange, California, responded, "Are we being creative enough in the sense of staying on top of changing technology and how people, young people especially, are communicating these days?"

Fr. William Hammer of St. Joseph Proto-Cathedral in Bardstown, Kentucky, expressed this concern well: "We've got to find a way to tap into social media better, especially to tap into ways of using the Internet to reach our younger adults—the twenty- to thirty- to forty-year-olds. But I think that's a huge opportunity and we're just not yet tapping into that. It's an opportunity and a challenge."

Fr. Henry Petter of St. Ann parish in Coppell, Texas, said, "To reach the younger people—our ministry is doing that right now very well, through technology and communication, but we still have a long way to go."

Handled well, technology has the potential to revitalize the entire mission of the Church. Christian missiologist Ed Stetzer wrote a compelling piece for *Christianity Today* in which he identified three major components of church life that technology can empower: communication, community, and discipleship.[28]

COMMUNICATION

Although, as with all technology, online communication misses the element of physical interaction, it is still direct and clear. It allows a parish to provide communication and support that can be tailored to the various ages and stages of parishioners' lives, making church meaningful and relevant even for those who are homebound, away on travel, or raising young children.

To reach a generation that is linked through Facebook, Twitter, and other platforms, one parish we spoke with created a technology task force, employing a young parishioner to go out to nondenominational parishes to discover how they used technology. This parish then decided what would work from a Catholic perspective and implemented the changes.

Fr. Tim Fitzgerald of SS. John and Paul parish in Altoona, Iowa, weighed his options aloud:

> It no longer works to simply open the doors and expect people to show up. I think it calls for a real different disposition and mentality. In a sense we have to go out to people far more than [we had to] twenty years in the past. That's a big factor. I think the switch to electronic-based resources and communications is a very helpful tool with all of that. It's hard to keep up with it, but [we are trying] to keep pressing ahead with parish resources online—for instance, faith formation resources online for the parish.

COMMUNITY

Today's communities are not dependent on proximity. Technology has eliminated the need for people to physically be near each other in order to connect. "We really just keep using social media very aggressively to invite people and inform people about what we're doing," reported Fr. Marcel Taillon of St. Thomas More parish in Narragansett, Rhode Island.

> It's part of our evangelical outreach, and I value that. That's why our website is always up to date. . . . It's got color photos every week of different people and their names, pictures of the CCD classes and the teachers, and it creates community because people see all the hidden ministries that are happening in the parish— the money counters and the stuff that never gets any

press. So that's what we do: we try to affirm the people and show the ministries that no one sees. We do that pretty regularly and pretty well.

While these regular posts may not garner massive attention immediately, over time they attract more and more eyeballs and engagement, especially among tech-aware millennials.

Sometimes this extended, online community can be more active than a physical one. Introverted individuals and parishioners who never connected before can take active roles in their parish community through online interaction. When people who feel more comfortable interacting online become accustomed to being engaged via their digital community, they may eventually become more involved in the physical parish community as well. One suburban parish we spoke with wanted to start a group for young adults in their twenties and thirties. Instead of facing the uphill battle of making it happen at the church, they broke the ice with an online community. The parish is now looking for ways to help these digital community members feel more a part of the larger parish community.

DISCIPLESHIP

Technology itself is not the goal. The goal is always to deepen discipleship and create new disciples. In this way, technology is a tool for evangelization. As Fr. Jack Gleason of the Church of St. Mary in Tulsa, Oklahoma, articulated:

> In terms of going deeper with our youth, again, the cultural influences for them, and keeping them engaged, a great challenge is: How do we meet young people where they are and help them take the next step? There are so many things they're involved in, and really, [we are] competing with all the electronic things that entertain people. If you can get them to have just one meaningful experience, they'll see something deeper, and they'll want more.

Our research offers actions that have yielded success in reaching millennials and other young adults through dialogue, mentorship, leadership, and technology. Although neither we nor the pastors in our dataset tested these models on different age and affinity groups, there is no reason to assume that these models are limited to connecting with millennials; they may very well be equally applicable to other groups.

CHALLENGES RECAPPED

1. American Catholics are unaccustomed and resistant to evangelizing.

2. As a result of the dramatic decline in religious affiliation in the United States, new attitudes and methods of evangelization must be developed.

3. Millennials are a multifaceted population who live with great uncertainty and anxiety. The Church must develop new ways of making church relevant to them through dialogue, mentoring, and opportunities for leadership.

4. Technology has the potential to revitalize the mission of the Church, but the Church has been slow to adapt to it.

EPILOGUE

This book has been a joy and a challenge to research and write. It has been a pleasure to work with our Parish Catalyst team as we interviewed, analyzed, and organized these past two years. And it has been a privilege and an inspiration to speak with many dynamic pastors.

Poring over the data, we gleaned findings and conclusions that sometimes made perfect intuitive sense and other times did not. Ultimately our findings fit comfortably into four themes: sharing leadership, growing spiritually, worshiping, and reaching out. To us these four areas neatly encompass the principal aspects of parish life. The pastoral orientation that connects these four themes can be captured in three words: collaborative, intentional, and joyful.

It was important to all of us that the material set forth here could withstand strict academic scrutiny. In the secular culture that we live in, religion in general and the Catholic Church in particular are too often dismissed as outdated and even worse. We have often been attacked in an anecdotal or episodic fashion—all the more reason why our content should be academically airtight. So we made sure that our research was conducted in a comprehensive way, much as any academic work would require. We believe we have satisfied that strict standard, which pushed us continually to test and probe to make sure we didn't come up short in a technical sense. We hope you agree.

Time and time again we were inspired to hear about the incredibly important work pastors and their staffs at these vibrant parishes are doing with measurable results, sometimes under very difficult circumstances. Our pastors and their staffs are the heroes of this book.

Quite honestly, my fondest hope was that this book would be more than just another academic study. I wanted to send a message of hope and optimism, grounded in realism: there are parishes in our Church where important and meaningful work is being done every single day and quantifiable progress is being achieved; we have every reason to believe that the future is bright in this critical American arena of Catholicism—the parish—where 80 percent of our members observe their faith.

So let us return now to where we began: my own parish in Santa Monica.

I'm listening. My back pockets are parked in a wooden pew. Despite the firmness, I can't think of a more comfortable seat to listen from.

"We are celebrating today this wonderful feast of Pentecost. It's an incredible opportunity to reflect on that first reading from the Acts of the Apostles."

My pastor walks slowly down the center aisle of the church.

"The thing that most of us remember about Pentecost is the gift of tongues."

I sling my shoulder over the back of the pew and push my glasses closer to the bridge of my nose. I prepare to hear Beethoven in my backyard.

"But the thing that we forget—at least I forget— is that it's not just the gift of speaking this new language to people. It's also the great gift of hearing."

I look at a couple in front of me. A young boy is climbing on his mother as though she's a piece of playground equipment. He is not paying attention and she is struggling to, but that's okay. Msgr. Torgerson is about to make her task easier.

My pastor always tells a story, and today is no different:

> More than a century ago, a great sailing ship was
> stranded off the coast of South America. Week after

week, the ship lay there in still waters with not a hint of breeze. The captain was desperate, and the crew was dying of thirst. Then, in the far horizon, a steamship appeared heading directly toward them.

As it drew near, the captain called out, "We need water! Give us water!"

After a silence that felt like an eternity, someone on the steamship shouted back, "Lower your buckets where you are!"

The captain was furious. He called again: "Please give us some water, we are dying of thirst!"

The steamer gave the same reply: "Lower your buckets where you are." With that, the steamship sailed away.

The captain was beside himself. His anger turned into despair. He did not know what to do. He wandered the boat, lost and hopeless. Eventually, he went below the deck. There he watched a haggard row man shaking violently as he lowered a bucket into the sea. The captain then watched this man taste what was hoisted up.

The second the water hit this man's lips, the captain knew: it was perfectly sweet, fresh water.

It turns out, the ship was just outside the mouth of the Amazon River for all of those weeks. All along, they had been sitting right on top of all the fresh water they ever needed.

The rest of the Mass flows by the way so many have for me over the past twenty-five years at St. Monica's: the warm peace offerings and the myriad faces of the two-thousand-year-old Communion line. As Mass concludes, I step out the side door and into the fading southern California sunshine.

People spill out over the front steps of the church as I round the corner. They are the same steps I used to have to drag my small children up more than two decades ago. I feel a smile stretch across my face.

No matter what is going on in my life or in the world at large, it's a very rare day that I hear Msgr. Torgerson and don't feel uplifted. As I reach for the door of my car, the final words of today's sermon are ringing in my head: "What we are really seeking is already inside us, waiting to be discovered and waiting to be embraced. The Holy Spirit of God, who has been living within us since the moment of our Baptism, the Holy Spirit is saying to us at this very moment, from deep in our hearts, 'Lower your buckets right where you are—taste and see.'"

APPENDIXES

Parish Catalyst recognizes that all Catholic parishes seek to understand the needs of today's world, reflect on those needs in light of the Gospel and our tradition, and respond in ways that serve God's people. We appreciate that for various reasons some pastors and parishes are better equipped than others to find creative and adaptive responses to those needs. Our goal was to identify these "islands of strength," encourage their continued growth and development, and help share their insights with others. This research thus sought to capture the state of the most energized and vibrant Catholic parishes we could find. The study was designed to elicit information from pastors about their parish's greatest strengths, most exciting opportunities, and most pressing challenges.

We believe that our study was unique in our beloved Catholic tradition from the standpoint of our response rate (82 percent), as well as our process and protocol, including identification of participants, data collection procedures, and the intensive staged data analysis process and coding. Further information on each of these areas is available on our website www.parishcatalyst.org.

APPENDIX A

DESCRIPTIVE STATISTICS

In this appendix, we present descriptive statistics about the pastors and parishes in the sample. For additional information visit ParishCatalyst.org.

Table A.1 shows information about the pastors we interviewed. The average age of the pastors in our dataset, 59.6 years old, was slightly lower than the average age of all Catholic priests, 63 years old.[1] Table A.2 contains data about the parishes we surveyed.

Table A.1 Pastor characteristics

	Age at time of interview	Number of years ordained	Number of years at current parish
Range	33–84	4–57	<1–39
Average	59.6	30.1	9.7
Median	61	30	8

Table A.2 Parish characteristics

	Annual Offertory	Number of Registered Households*	Weekly Mass Attendance	Offertory / Mass Attendance [average offering per Mass]	Attendance [average attendance per household] Registered Households
Range	$58,000–$5,000,000	100 – 9,300 HHs	150 – 8,500 People	$83–$5,600	0.125 – 4.00
Average	$1,221,761	2,386 HHs	2104 People	$658	0.98
Median	$1,000,000	1,919 HHs	1,764 People	$577	0.90

* The Catholic Church tends to measure parish size by registered households rather than by individual parishioners. Although some use a general multiplier to extrapolate the number of parishioners from the number of families (e.g., "x3"), this can be difficult in parishes with, for example, a large percentage of elderly parishioners.

Though our pastors reported quite a range of annual offertories and registered households, there were more than a few parishes with many families or large offertories. Half of the pastors we interviewed served parishes with annual offertories of more than $1 million, and half served parishes with more than 1,919 registered households. The pastors of our dataset came from larger and better funded parishes than the national average. The average number of registered households per parish for all American Catholic parishes is 1,168, and the average offertory is just shy of $700,000.[2]

Figure A.1 and figure A.2 illustrate the distribution of registered households and annual offertories more clearly. Parishes of 1,000 to 1,999 registered households occurred most frequently in our dataset. In terms of annual offertory, parishes with offertories of $500,000 to $999,000 occurred most frequently, numbering almost sixty.

Figure A.3 shows the regional representation of the parishes in our dataset, which more or less matches parish distribution across the country. The Northeast and Midwest have the largest percentage of

Figure A.1 Distribution of number of registered households in dataset parishes

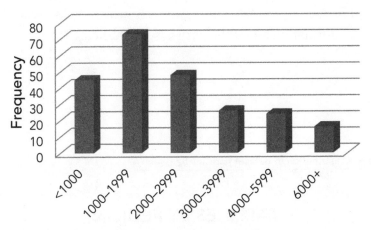

HOW MANY REGISTERED HOUSEHOLDS DOES YOUR PARISH HAVE?

Figure A.2 Annual recorded offertories in dataset parishes

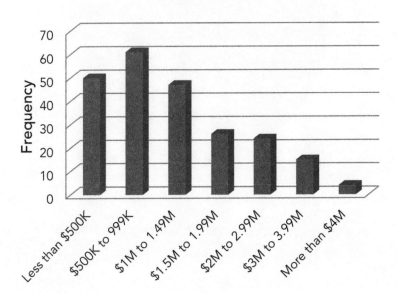

WHAT IS YOUR PARISH'S ANNUAL OFFERTORY?

parishes (30 percent each), with the South and West splitting the remainder, with 20 percent of parishes each. Per *The Official Catholic Directory 2013*, 37 percent of all parishes are in the Midwest, with 27 percent in the Northeast, 22 percent in the South, and 14 percent in the West.[3]

Figure A.4, figure A.5, and figure A.6 provide additional demographic information about the parishes we studied.

Figure A.3 Distribution of dataset parishes by region

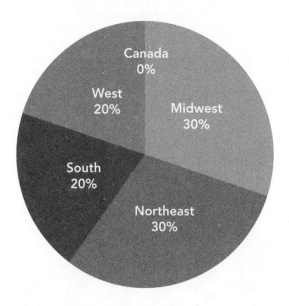

PARISHES BY REGION

Figure A.4 Distribution of dataset parishes by neighborhood type

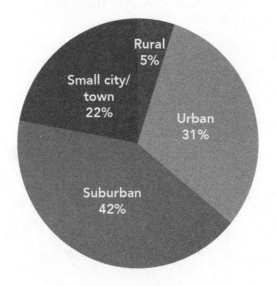

WHAT TYPE OF NEIGHBORHOOD
SURROUNDS THE PARISH?

Rural
5%

Small city/
town
22%

Urban
31%

Suburban
42%

Figure A.5 Data on school affiliations of dataset parishes

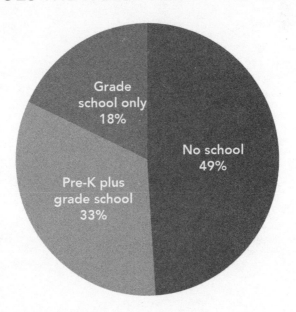

DOES THE PARISH HAVE A SCHOOL?

Grade
school only
18%

No school
49%

Pre-K plus
grade school
33%

Figure A.6 Dataset parishes reporting on parishioner race or ethnicity

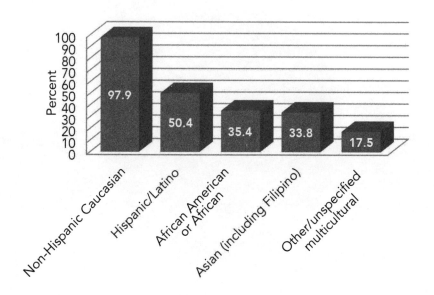

PERCENTAGE OF PARISHES REPORTING PARISHONERS OF EACH RACE OR ETHNICITY

APPENDIX B

STRENGTHS, OPPORTUNITIES, AND CHALLENGES

Qualitative coding in NVivo10 data analysis software allowed us to rigorously and systematically track which themes were present or absent in each interview, which themes occurred the most frequently, and which themes were framed by the pastors as strengths, opportunities, and challenges. For example, 90 percent of the pastors considered spiritual growth and discipleship to be strengths of their parishes.

The following numbers indicate the percentages of pastors who considered a particular theme or characteristic to be a *strength* at their parish:

Spiritual Growth and Discipleship	90
Leadership Development	80
Liturgy	75
Community	73
Stewardship and Generosity	69
Staff	68
Finances	67
Service/Social Justice/Diversity/Helping Poor	63
Welcoming and Hospitality	61
Evangelization/Reaching/Missions	49
Music	48
Facilities and Architecture	47
Young Adults	33
Technology	17

The following numbers indicate the percentages of pastors who considered a particular theme or characteristic to be an *opportunity* at their parish:

Spiritual Growth and Discipleship	77
Evangelization/Reaching/Missions	59
Leadership Development	35
Service/Social Justice/Diversity/Helping Poor	35
Facilities and Architecture	34
Young Adults	32
Staff	28
Welcoming and Hospitality	27
Stewardship and Generosity	19
Technology	16
Liturgy	11
Music	9

The following numbers indicate the percentages of pastors who considered a particular theme or characteristic to be a *challenge* at their parish:

Secularism and Competing Priorities	71
Spiritual Growth and Discipleship	70
Finances	54
Staff	45
Church Hierarchy	45
Leadership Development	38
Facilities and Architecture	37
Young Adults	34
Community	33
Service/Social Justice/Diversity/Helping Poor	31
Evangelization/Reaching/Missions	27
Liturgy	14
Technology	11
Welcoming and Hospitality	9
Music	8

NOTES

INTRODUCTION

1. United States Conference of Catholic Bishops, *Communities of Salt and Light: Reflection on the Social Mission of the Parish*, http://www.usccb.org/beliefs-and-teachings/what-we-believe/catholic-social-teaching/communities-of-salt-and-light-reflections-on-the-social-mission-of-the-parish.cfm.

2. Bob habitually underemphasizes the level of forethought he puts into his projects; there was nothing arbitrary or ad hoc about Leadership Network's ministry under his direction.

3. Norman K. Denzin and Yvonna S. Lincoln, *The SAGE Handbook of Qualitative Research*, 4th ed. (New York: Sage Publications, 2011).

4. Data on the distribution of the parishes in our dataset can be found in table A.2 (page 182).

5. The pastors in our dataset ranged in age from thirty-three to eighty-four years old. The comparable average figure for all Catholic pastors is sixty-three years, as seen in Mary L. Gautier, Paul M. Perl, and Stephen J. Fichter, *Same Call, Different Men: The Evolution of the Priesthood since Vatican II* (Collegeville, MN: Liturgical Press, 2011), 3.

6. James T. Fisher, *Catholics in America*, Religion in American Life (Oxford: Oxford University Press, 2001), 30.

7. Ibid., 33–34.

8. Ibid.

9. Ibid., 37.

10. Ibid.

11. Molly Worthen, "American Christianity and Secularism at a Crossroads," *New York Times*, December 22, 2012, http://www.nytimes.com/2012/12/23/opinion/sunday/american-christianity-and-secularism-at-a-crossroads.html.

12. Fisher, *Catholics in America*, 46–49.

13. Ibid.

14. Ibid., 82.

15. Jay P. Dolan, *The American Catholic Parish: A History from 1850 to the Present,* vol. 1, *Northeast, Southeast, South Central* (Mahwah, NJ: Paulist Press, 1987), 12.

16. Ibid.

17. Fisher, *Catholics in America,* 78.

18. Ibid., 79.

19. Dolan, *American Catholic Parish,* 13.

20. Ibid., 2.

21. Ibid., 3.

22. Ibid., 9.

23. The Northeast remains the population center of American Catholicism today.

24. William V. D'Antonio, James D. Davidson, Dean R. Hoge, and Ruth A. Wallace, *Laity: American and Catholic: Transforming the Church* (Kansas City, MO: Sheed and Ward, 1996), 2.

25. Dolan, *American Catholic Parish,* 86.

26. Ibid., 22.

27. Fisher, *Catholics in America,* 87.

28. Ibid.

29. Dolan, *American Catholic Parish,* 24.

30. Ibid.

31. Ibid., 60.

32. Ibid., 61.

33. John Tracy Ellis, *American Catholicism* (Chicago: University of Chicago Press, 1969), 124.

34. Ibid., 134.

35. R. Scott Appleby, review of *The American Catholic Parish: A History from 1850 to the Present,* by Jay P. Dolan, *Church History: Studies in Christianity and Culture* 58, no. 2 (June 1989): 268–70.

36. Dolan, *American Catholic Parish,* 67.

37. Catholic World Report, "The Rise, Fall, and Future of Catholicism in the US," *The Catholic World Report,* May 10, 2013, http://www.catholicworldreport.com/Item/2247/the_rise_fall_and_future_of_catholicism_in_the_us.aspx.

38. Peter Steinfels, *A People Adrift: The Crisis of the Roman Catholic Church in America* (New York: Simon and Schuster, 2004), 4.

39. Justices Alito, Kennedy, Roberts, Scalia, Thomas, and Sotomayor were all Catholic.

40. PEW statistics vary somewhat from CARA's statistics for 2015. CARA reported that in 2015 there were 81.6 million survey-based, self-identifying Catholics in the United States, or 25.5 percent of the US population in 2015. CARA also reported that the *Official Catholic Directory* stated that there were 68.1 million parish-connected Catholics, or 21.28 percent of the US population in 2015.

41. Center for Applied Research in the Apostolate (CARA), "Frequently Requested Church Statistics," accessed September 9, 2015, http://cara.georgetown.edu/frequently-requested-church-statistics.

42. Pew Research Center, "America's Changing Religious Landscape," May 12, 2015, http://www.pewforum.org/files/2015/05/RLS-08-26-full-report.pdf, 3.

43. https://en.wikipedia.org/wiki/Settlements_and_bankruptcies_in_Catholic_sex_abuse_cases.

44. CARA, "Frequently Requested Church Statistics."

1. THE NOT-SO-LONE RANGER

1. Of the 244 interviewees, seventy-six mentioned Pope Francis.

2. The pastor is the "administrator of the goods of the parish." John P. Beal, James A. Coriden, and Thomas J. Green, *New Commentary on the Code of Canon Law* (Mahwah, NJ: Paulist Press, 2000), 704.

3. Jim Collins, *Good to Great: Why Some Companies Make the Leap . . . and Others Don't* (New York: HarperCollins, 2001), 13.

4. Similar findings of pastor leadership styles were also documented in Marti R. Jewell and David A. Ramey, *The Changing Face of Church: Emerging Models of Parish Leadership* (Chicago: Loyola Press, 2010), 94–100.

5. Although not addressed by the pastors in our study, it is important to note that along with the development of lay ministers, the permanent deaconate was also reestablished by the Second Vatican Council. CARA reports that in 2005, 18,802 permanent deacons were also serving the church.

6. The number fifty-one is comprised of 21 percent of respondents, nineteen of whom discussed their spiritual director and thirty-two of whom discussed their priest support group.

2. CHALLENGES OF SHARED LEADERSHIP

1. The fact that 30 percent of pastors sleep very well is noteworthy in and of itself. My guess is that it is due in no small part to the fact that they have dedicated their lives to helping others.

2. Gallup's StrengthsFinder assessment tool helps people discover their unique combination of skills, talents, and knowledge—also known as strengths. http://www.strengthsfinder.com/home.aspx.

3. Warren Bennis, *BrainyQuote.com*, accessed April 16, 2016, http://www.brainyquote.com/quotes/authors/w/warren_bennis_2.html.

4. Warren Bennis, *GoodReads*, accessed April 27, 2016, http://www.goodreads.com/4993165.Warren_G_Bennis.

5. Mark M. Gray, Mary L. Gautier, and Melissa A. Cidade, *The Changing Face of US Catholic Parishes* (Washington, DC: National Association for Lay Ministry, 2011), http://cara.georgetown.edu/staff/webpages/Parishes%20Phase%20One.pdf, 7.

6. CARA, "Frequently Requested Church Statistics."

7. Gray, Gautier, and Cidade, *The Changing Face of US Catholic Parishes*, 20.

8. These include but are not limited to Catholic Leadership Institute (CLI), Amazing Parish, and Parish Catalyst.

9. CARA, "Frequently Requested Church Statistics."

10. Mark Gray, "Facing a Future with Fewer Catholic Priests," *Our Sunday Visitor Newsweekly*, June 16, 2010, https://www.osv.com/OSVNewsweekly/ByIssue/Article/TabId/735/ArtMID/13636/ArticleID/4248/Facing-a-future-with-fewer-Catholic-priests.aspx.

11. CARA, "Frequently Requested Church Statistics."

12. Mark M. Gray, ed., "Rise of the Million Dollar Parish," *Nineteen Sixty-Four* (blog), July 25, 2014, http://nineteensixty-four.blogspot.com/2014/07/rise-of-million-dollar-parish.html.

13. Ibid.

14. Ibid. "Revenue" includes the regular offertory, special collections, and subsidies.

3. YEARNING FOR MORE

1. A disciple may be usefully distinguished from an apostle. *Apostle* means "missionary, sender, emissary." Both disciples and apostles have a heart for Christ and are interested in deepening their personal relationships with Christ. However, apostles also reach out to others. They are externally focused, keen on sharing the Good News with other people and helping them develop a heart for Christ. Apostles are, in a sense, the focus of part IV of this book.

2. Barna Group, "The State of Discipleship" (Colorado Springs, CO: NavPress, 2015), 18.

3. Cally Parkinson and Nancy Scammacca Lewis, *Rise: Bold Strategies to Transform Your Church* (Colorado Springs, CO: NavPress, 2015), xi.

4. A similar option is Cornerstone, a retreat program offered separately for men and women.

5. Cursillo takes place over a three-day weekend with the goal of training Christian leaders. Cursillo stresses personal spiritual development, and provides follow-up reunions.

6. Alpha International, accessed April 26, 2016, http://www.alphausa.org/about.

7. Word on Fire, accessed April 27, 2016, http://www.wordonfire.org/resources/studyprogram/catholicism-student-study-guide-and-workbook/2372.

8. ChristLife, accessed April 27, 2016, https://christlife.org/christlife-series/discovering-christ.

9. Parish Success Group, accessed April 27, 2016, http://www.parishsuccess-group.com/about.

10. The Generations of Faith approach includes intergenerational, catechetical programs for all ages and resources for home faith-sharing and learning. Not considered a program, Generations of Faith is an approach to creating life-long intergenerational, events-centered faith formation.

11. Like the Adoration statistic presented later, this is a baseline. There may be more parishes in the sample that have small groups. We did not ask, "Do you have small groups?" as part of the standard protocol. This figure represents the percentage of pastors who brought up small groups as important parts of their ministries.

12. Like the Adoration and small groups statistics, this is a baseline. There may be more parishes in the sample that have missions. We did not ask, "Do you have missions?" as part of the standard protocol. This figure represents the percentage of pastors who brought up missions as important parts of their ministries.

13. It was noteworthy to our staff that Adoration came up unsolicited in many of our interviews. We believe that the number of parishes in our dataset that offer Adoration may well be higher since there was no reference to Adoration in our interview protocol.

4. CHALLENGES TO ENGAGEMENT, SPIRITUAL MATURITY, AND DISCIPLESHIP

1. Pew Research Center, "Faith in Flux," April 27, 2009, http://www.pewforum.org/2009/04/27/faith-in-flux/.

2. For the purpose of this discussion, we are setting aside the 25 percent figure from Willow Creek, since it includes congregants of many religious faiths. All of the other percentages in the table relate to Catholics specifically.

3. CARA, "Frequently Requested Church Statistics." The 68.1 million cited by CARA comes from the 2015 Official Catholic Directory, which includes Baptisms, parish rolls.

4. True value proposition comes from seeing opportunities other people do not and turning them into success.

5. A VIBRANT SUNDAY EXPERIENCE

1. Michael White and Tom Corcoran, *Rebuilt: Awakening the Faithful, Reaching the Lost, and Making Church Matter* (Notre Dame, IN: Ave Maria Press, 2013), 87.

2. Austin Flannery, ed. *"Lumen Gentium," Documents of Vatican II* (Northport, NY: Costello, 1998), 11.

3. See page 67.

4. The seven parishes that upgraded their websites were Catholic Community of St. Francis of Assisi, (www.stfrancisraleigh.org), Old St. Patrick's Church (www.old-stpats.org), the Parish Community of St. Helen (www.sainthelen.org), St. Benedict (www.saintbenedict.ca), St. Camillus, a Catholic Multicultural Parish (www.stcamill-luschurch.org), St. Peter-St. Denis Church (spyonkers.com), and St. Monica Catholic Community (stmonica.net).

5. A narthex is an antechamber or gathering space in the front of a church. An architectural element associated with early Christian and Byzantine basilicas, it is traditionally located at the west end of the nave, opposite the church's main altar and sometimes separated from the nave by a screen or a rail. In modern churches, the narthex may be indoors (like a lobby) or outdoors (like a front porch).

6. Karla J. Bellinger, *Connecting Pulpit and Pew: Breaking Open the Conversation about Catholic Preaching* (Collegeville, MN: Liturgical Press, 2014), 6.

7. Catholic Leadership Institute, Disciple Maker Index. CLI partnered with a survey data firm called Measuring Success to design and administer a survey of Catholic parishioners in the United States. They created a metric called the Disciple Maker Index, which shows what characteristics of parishes are most strongly associated with discipleship. Parishioners were invited to complete an email survey with questions about their satisfaction with their parish and pastor, how likely they are to recommend their parish to others, and details about how often they participate in various parish activities. http://www.catholicleaders.org/home.aspx?pagename=SupportingSpecialProjects.

6. CHALLENGES TO EXCELLENT SUNDAYS

1. Pew Research Center, "America's Changing Religious Landscape," 35.

2. Ibid., 40.

3. Tim Padgett, "Why So Many Latinos Are Leaving Catholicism— And Religion Altogether" *WLRN*, May 28, 2014, http://wlrn.org/post/why-so-many-latinos-are-leaving-catholicism-and-religion-altogether.

4. Emma Green, "The Catholic Church Isn't Doing So Well with Hispanic-Americans," *The Atlantic*, May 7, 2014, http://www.theatlantic.com/national/

archive/2014/05/the-catholic-church-isnt-doing-great-with-hispanic-americans/361709/.

5. Ibid.

6. Isaac Chotiner, "Secularism Is Good for America—Especially Christians," *New Republic,* February 10, 2014, http://www.newrepublic.com/article/116509/secularism-america-good-everyone-including-christians.

7. Pew Research Center, "America's Changing Religious Landscape," 3.

8. Cary Funk and Greg Smith, "'Nones' on the Rise: New Report Finds One-in-Five Adults Have No Religious Affiliation," Pew Research Center, October 9, 2012, http://www.pewforum.org/2012/10/09/nones-on-the-rise-new-report-finds-one-in-five-adults-have-no-religious-affiliation/.

9. Ibid.

10. It may be worth noting, nonetheless, that church membership and attendance peaked in 1963, before which (from the beginning of the twentieth century through World War II) membership and attendance had done no more than "keep pace with population growth." What we are seeing now in the Church, then, is not a "rise and fall" so much as different phases of a dynamic cycle. See Charles Murray, *Coming Apart: The State of White America, 1960–2010* (New York: Crown Forum, 2013), 206.

11. One parish in the Midwest offered babysitting and a date night for young married couples living on a tight budget. Others developed homily series that targeted work, family, and social concerns.

7. ENTERING THE MISSION FIELD

1. United States Conference of Catholic Bishops, *Go and Make Disciples: A National Plan and Strategy for Catholic Evangelization in the United States* (Washington DC: USCCB, 2012), http://www.usccb.org/beliefs-and-teachings/how-we-teach/evangelization/go-and-make-disciples/go-and-make-disciples-a-national-plan-and-strategy-for-catholic-evangelization-in-the-united-states.cfm.

2. Ibid., "Our Goals," par. 46.

3. Sir Edward V. Appleton was an English physicist, Nobel Prize winner, and pioneer in radio physics.

4. This discussion is adapted from a message posted by the Most Reverend John C. Wester, Bishop of the Catholic Diocese of Salt Lake City, to the diocesan website http://ddd.dioslc.org in 2015.

5. Richard Rohr, "The Parable of the Life Saving Station," YouTube video, 5:39, Center for Action and Contemplation, January 27, 2009, http://www.youtube.com/watch?v=TNeuVHdbog4.

6. Others have published on this subject previously, notably Robert S. Rivers, *From Maintenance to Mission: Evangelization and the Revitalization of the Parish*

(Mahwah, NJ: Paulist Press, 2005), and Craig L. Nessan, *Beyond Maintenance to Mission: A Theology of the Congregation* (Minneapolis, MN: Fortress Press, 2010).

7. Barna defines the unchurched as "someone who has not attended a Christian church service, other than a special event such as a wedding or funeral, at any time during the past six months." Barna Group, *Churchless: Understanding Today's Unchurched and How to Connect with Them*, ed. George Barna and David Kinnaman (Carol Stream, IL: Tyndale Momentum, 2014), 6.

8. Ibid., 158.

8. CHALLENGES TO EVANGELIZATION

1. "In . . . the spring of 2004, John C. Haughey, S.J., noted that many of his non-Catholic students are not shy about making personal faith statements, both in the classroom and outside. Catholic students, on the other hand, seldom do so. These Catholic young people will talk about church issues and controversies or about moral values, but not about their relationship with Christ or about how they recognize God's action in their life." Martin Pable, "Why Don't Catholics Share Their Faith?" *America*, September 19, 2005, http://americamagazine.org/issue/542/article/why-dont-catholics-share-their-faith.

2. Isaac Hecker (1819–1888) was a missionary, an author, and the founder of the Paulists. Hecker was much in demand as a lecturer and exponent of Catholic truth. For years he was eagerly welcomed by overflowing crowds in New York, Boston, Detroit, St. Louis, Chicago, and other large cities. "Isaac Thomas Hecker," *The Catholic Encyclopedia*, accessed August 17, 2015, http://www.newadvent.org/cathen/07186a.htm.

3. Dean R. Hoge, William D. Dinges, Mary Johnson, and Juan L. Gonzales Jr., *Young Adult Catholics: Religion in the Culture of Choice* (Notre Dame, IN: University of Notre Dame Press, 2001), 7.

4. "In addition, the civil rights movement cast many clergy, nuns, and parishioners, energized by Vatican II, into new social roles and relationships with far reaching implications for the Church's own internal life." Ibid., 11.

5. "The Church, therefore, urges her sons to enter with prudence and charity into discussion and collaboration with members of other religions. Let Christians, while witnessing to their own faith and way of life, acknowledge, preserve and encourage the spiritual and moral truths found among non-Christians, also their social life and culture." Paul VI, *Nostra Aetate,* accessed April 29, 2016, http://www.vatican.va/archive/hist_councils/ii_vatican_council/documents/vat-ii_decl_19651028_nostra-aetate_en.html.

6. George Weigel, *Evangelical Catholicism: Deep Reform in the 21st-Century Church* (New York: Basic Books, 2013), 19.

7. Pew Research Center, "America's Changing Religious Landscape," 20.

8. Ibid., 13.

9. Ibid., 11.

10. Richard Fry, "This Year, Millennials Will Overtake Baby Boomers" Pew Research Center, January 16, 2015, http://www.pewresearch.org/fact-tank/2015/01/16/this-year-millennials-will-overtake-baby-boomers/.

11. Caleb Bislow, "Reaching the Millennial Tribe," *Unusual Soldiers* (blog), April 7, 2015, http://unusualsoldiers.org/exploring-and-reaching-the-millenial-tribe/.

12. David P. Setran and Chris A. Kiesling, *Spiritual Formation in Emerging Adulthood: A Practical Theology for College and Young Adult Ministry* (Grand Rapids, MI: Baker Academic, 2013), 2.

13. Ibid., 3.

14. On average Millennials rate their stress level at 5.4 out of 10, while the researchers consider a rating of 3.6 or lower to be healthy. Tracy Miller, "Young, Broke, and Stressed Out: Millennials Feel More Anxious and Less Able to Cope than Older Adults, Survey Finds," *Daily News*, February 7, 2013, http://www.nydailynews.com/life-style/health/millennials-feel-stressed-older-adults-article-1.1258297.

15. Ibid. Previous generations are also changing as a result of technology. The effect that technology has on our thinking, our relationships, and our understanding of the world cannot be overstated.

16. Muhammad Yunus, *BrainyQuote.com*, accessed April 28, 2016, http://www.brainyquote.com/quotes/quotes/m/muhammadyu228663.html. Muhammad Yunus is a Bangladeshi social entrepreneur, banker, economist, and civil society leader who was awarded the Nobel Peace Prize for founding the Grameen Bank and pioneering the concepts of microcredit and microfinance.

17. Wade Clark Roof and Mary Johnson, "Baby Boomers and the Return to the Churches," in *Church and Denominational Growth: What Does (and Does Not) Cause Growth or Decline*, ed. David A. Roozen and C. Kirk Hadaway (Nashville, TN: Abingdon, 1993), accessed August 3, 2015, http://hirr.hartsem.edu/bookshelf/Church&Denomgrowth/ch&dngrw-ch14.pdf.

18. Barna Group, "Five Myths about Young Adult Church Dropouts," November 15, 2011, https://www.barna.org/millennials/534-five-myths-about-young-adult-church-dropouts#.V3GDgKJpGr8.

19. Ibid.

20. Ibid.

21. Barna Group, *Churchless*, 90.

22. In 2011, Barna Group interviewed 1,296 Christian (Catholic and Protestant) young adults ages eighteen to twenty-nine years old. David Kinnaman and Aly Hawkins, *You Lost Me: Why Young Adults Are Leaving the Church . . . And Rethinking Faith* (Grand Rapids, MI: Baker Books, 2011), 79.

23. Barna Group, *Making Space for Millennials*, 40.

24. Bislow, "Reaching the Millennial Tribe."

25. Ibid.

26. Barna Group, *Making Space for Millennials*, 48.

27. Ed Stetzer, "3 Ways Technology Enables the Mission of the Church," *Christianity Today, The Exchange* (blog), October 27, 2014, http://www.christianitytoday.com/edstetzer/2014/october/3-ways-technology-enables-mission-of-church.html.

28. Ibid.

APPENDIX A: DESCRIPTIVE STATISTICS

1. Gautier, Perl, and Fichter, *Same Call, Different Men*, 3, 43.

2. Gray, Gautier, and Cidade, *The Changing Face of US Catholic Parishes*, 17, 43.

3. Ibid., 17.

BIBLIOGRAPHY

Allen, John L. "What's This 'New Evangelization' Thing, Anyway?" *National Catholic Reporter*, March 7, 2013. http://ncronline.org/blogs/ncr-today/whats-new-evangelization-thing-anyway.

Appleby, R. Scott. Review of *The American Catholic Parish: A History from 1850 to the Present*, by Jay P. Dolan. *Church History: Studies in Christianity and Culture* 58, no. 2 (June 1989).

Barna Group. *Churchless: Understanding Today's Unchurched and How to Connect with Them*. Edited by George Barna and David Kinnaman. Carol Stream, IL: Tyndale Momentum, 2014.

———. "Five Myths about Young Adult Church Dropouts." November 15, 2011. http://www.barna.org/millennials/534-five-myths-about-young-adult-church-dropouts.

———. *Making Space for Millennials: A Blueprint for Your Culture, Ministry, Leadership and Facilities*. Ventura, CA: Barna Group, 2014.

———. *The State of Discipleship*. Colorado Springs, CO: NavPress, 2015.

Barron, Robert. *Catholicism: A Journey to the Heart of Faith*. Skokie, IL: Word on Fire Ministries, Image, 2011.

Beal, John P., James A. Coriden, and Thomas J. Green, eds. *New Commentary on the Code of Canon Law*. Mahwah, NJ: Paulist Press, 2000.

Bellinger, Karla J. *Connecting Pulpit and Pew: Breaking Open the Conversation about Catholic Preaching*. Collegeville, MN: Liturgical Press, 2014.

Bishops' Committee on Priestly Life and Ministry. *Fulfilled in Your Hearing: The Homily in the Sunday Assembly*. Washington, DC: USCCB, 2014.

Bislow, Caleb. "Reaching the Millennial Tribe." *Unusual Soldiers* (blog), April 7, 2015. http://unusualsoldiers.org/exploring-and-reaching-the-millenial-tribe/.

Catholic World Report, "The Rise, Fall, and Future of Catholicism in the US" *The Catholic World Report*, May 10, 2013. http://www.catholicworldreport.com/Item/2247/the_rise_fall_and_future_of_catholicism_in_the_us.aspx.

Center for Applied Research in the Apostolate. "Frequently Requested Church Statistics." Washington, DC: Center for Applied Research in the Apostolate, 2014. www.cara.georgetown.edu/frequently-requested-church-statistics.

Chotiner, Isaac. "Secularism Is Good for America—Especially Christians." *New Republic*, February 10, 2014. http://www.newrepublic.com/article/116509/secularism-america-good-everyone-including-christians.

Chrysostom, John. *On the Priesthood*. Translated by Graham Neville. Yonkers, NY: St. Vladimir Seminary Press, 1996.

Collins, Jim. *Good to Great: Why Some Companies Make the Leap . . . and Others Don't*. New York: HarperCollins, 2001.

D'Antonio, William, Michele Dillon, and Mary L. Gautier. *American Catholics in Transition*. Lanham, MD: Rowman and Littlefield, 2013.

Denzin, Norman K., and Yvonna S. Lincoln. *The SAGE Handbook of Qualitative Research*. 4th ed. Thousand Oaks, CA: SAGE Publications, 2011.

Dolan, Jay P. *The American Catholic Parish: A History from 1850 to the Present*, 2 vols. Mahwah, NJ: Paulist Press, 1987.

Dulles, Avery. *Church and Society*. New York: Fordham University Press, 2008.

Ellis, John Tracy. *American Catholicism*. The Chicago History of American Civilization, edited by Daniel J. Boorstin. Chicago: University of Chicago Press, 1956, 1961.

Fanning, Eileen. *Official Catholic Directory*. New Providence, NJ: National Register Publishing, 2013.

Fellowship of Catholic University Students. "What is the New Evangelization?" *FOCUS*, September 2012. http://www.focus.org/news-for-you/september/what-is-the-new-evangelization.html.

Fisher, James. *Catholics in America*. Religion in American Life. Oxford: Oxford University Press, 2000.

Flannery, Austin, ed. *Documents of Vatican II*. Northport, NY: Costello, 1998.

Fry, Richard. "This Year, Millennials Will Overtake Baby Boomers." Pew Research Center, January 16, 2015. http://www.pewform.org/2009/04/27/faith-in-flux.

Funk, Cary, and Greg Smith. "'Nones' on the Rise: One-in-Five Adults Have No Religious Affiliation." Pew Research Center, October 9, 2012. http://www.pewforum.org/2012/10/09/nones-on-the-rise-new-report-finds-one-in-five-adults-have-no-religious-affiliation/

Ganim, Carole, ed. *Shaping Catholic Parishes: Pastoral Leaders in the 21st Century*. Emerging Models of Pastoral Leadership. Chicago: Loyola Press, 2008.

Gautier, Mary L., Paul M. Perl, and Stephen J. Fichter. *Same Call, Different Men: The Evolution of the Priesthood since Vatican II*. Collegeville, MN: Liturgical Press, 2011.

Gray, Mark. "Facing a Future with Fewer Catholic Priests." *Our Sunday Visitor Newsweekly*, June 16, 2010. https://www.osv.com/OSVNewsweekly/ByIssue/Article/TabId/735/ArtMID/13636/ArticleID/4248/Facing-a-future-with-fewer-Catholic-priests.aspx.

Gray, Mark M., ed. "Rise of the Million Dollar Parish." *Nineteen Sixty-Four* (blog), July 25, 2014. http://nineteensixty-four.blogspot.com/2014/07/rise-of-million-dollar-parish.html.

Gray, Mark M., Mary L. Gautier, and Melissa A. Cidade. *The Changing Face of US Catholic Parishes*. Washington, DC: National Association for Lay Ministry, 2011. http://cara.georgetown.edu/staff/webpages/Parishes%20Phase%20One.pdf.

Green, Emma. "The Catholic Church Isn't Doing So Well With Hispanic Americans." *The Atlantic*, May 7, 2014.

Hawkins, Greg L., and Cally Parkinson. *Move: What 1,000 Churches Reveal About Spiritual Growth*. Grand Rapids, MI: Zondervan, 2011.

Hegy, Pierre. *Wake Up Lazarus! On Catholic Renewal.* Bloomington, IN: iUniverse, Inc., 2011.

Herbermann, Charles George. *The Catholic Encyclopedia.* Nashville, TN: Thomas Nelson, 2010.

Hoge, Dean R., William D. Dinges, Mary Johnson, and Juan L. Gonzales Jr. *Young Adult Catholics: Religion in the Culture of Choice.* Notre Dame, IN: University of Notre Dame Press, 2001.

Holmes, Paul A., ed. *A Pastor's Toolbox: Management Skills for Parish Leadership.* Collegeville, MN: Liturgical Press, 2010.

Jay, Meg. *The Defining Decade: Why Your Twenties Matter—And How to Make the Most of Them Now.* New York: Hachette Book Group, 2012.

Jewell, Marti R., and David A. Ramey. *The Changing Face of Church: Emerging Models of Parish Leadership.* Emerging Models of Pastoral Leadership. Chicago: Loyola Press, 2010.

Kelly, Matthew. *The Four Signs of a Dynamic Catholic.* Hebron, KY: Beacon Publishing, 2012.

———. *Rediscover Catholicism.* Hebron, KY: Beacon Publishing, 2010.

Kinnaman, David, and Aly Hawkins. *You Lost Me: Why Young Christians Are Leaving Church . . . And Rethinking Faith.* Grand Rapids, MI: Baker Books, 2011.

Mallon, James. *Divine Renovation: Bringing Your Parish from Maintenance to Mission.* New London, CT: Twenty-Third Publications, 2014.

Miller, Tracy. "Young, Broke, and Stressed Out: Millennials Feel More Anxious and Less Able to Cope than Older Adults, Survey Finds." *Daily News,* February 7, 2013. http://www.nydailynews.com/life-style/health/millennials-feel-stressed-older-adults-article-1.1258297.

Murray, Charles. *Coming Apart: The State of White America, 1960–2010.* New York: Crown Forum, 2012, 2013.

Nessan, Craig L. *Beyond Maintenance to Mission: A Theology of the Congregation.* Minneapolis, MN: Fortress Press, 2010.

Novak, Michael, and William E. Simon Jr. *Living the Call: An Introduction to the Lay Vocation.* New York: Encounter Books, 2011.

Pable, Martin. "Why Don't Catholics Share Their Faith?" *America,* September 19, 2005. http://americamagazine.org/issue/542/article/why-dont-catholics-share-their-faith.

Padgett, Tim. "Why So Many Latinos Are Leaving Catholicism—And Religion Altogether." *WLRN,* May 28, 2014. http://wlrn.org/post/why-so-many-latinos-are-leaving-catholicism-and-religion-altogether.

Parkinson, Cally, and Nancy Scammacca Lewis. *Rise: Bold Strategies to Transform Your Church.* Colorado Springs, CO: NavPress, 2015.

Pew Research Center. "America's Changing Religious Landscape." May 12, 2015. http://www.pewforum.org/files/2015/05/RLS-08-26-full-report.pdf.

———. "Faith in Flux." April 27, 2009. http://www.pewforum.org/2009/04/27/faith-in-flux.

Rivers, Robert S. *From Maintenance to Mission: Evangelization and the Revitalization of the Parish.* Mahwah, NJ: Paulist Press, 2005.

Roof, Wade Clark, and Mary Johnson. "Baby Boomers and the Return to the Church-es." In *Church and Denominational Growth: What Does (and Does Not) Cause Growth or Decline*, edited by David A. Roozen and C. Kirk Hadaway. Nashville, TN: Abingdon, 1993. Accessed August 3, 2015, http://hirr.hartsem.edu/book-shelf/Church&Denomgrowth/ch&dngrw-ch14.pdf

Schor, Juliet B. *The Overworked American: The Unexpected Decline of Leisure Time*. New York: Basic Books, 1992.

Setran, David P., and Chris A. Kiesling. *Spiritual Formation in Emerging Adult-hood: A Practical Theology for College and Young Adult Ministry*. Grand Rap-ids, MI: Baker Academic, 2013.

Steinfels, Peter. *A People Adrift: The Crisis of the Roman Catholic Church in Amer-ica*. New York: Simon and Schuster, 2003.

Stetzer, Ed. "Three Ways Technology Enables the Mission of the Church." *Christian-ity Today, The Exchange* (blog), October 2014. http://www.christianitytoday.com/edstetzer/2014/october/3-ways-technology-enables-mission-of-church.html.

United States Conference of Catholic Bishops, trans. *The Catechism of the Catholic Church*. New York and Mahwah, NJ: Paulist Press, 1994.

———. *Communities of Salt and Light: Reflection on the Social Mission of the Church*. Washington, DC: USCCB, 1996.

———. *Go and Make Disciples: A National Plan and Strategy for Catholic Evangeli-zation in the United States*, 10th Anniversary Edition. Washington, DC: USCCB, 2002.

Weddell, Sherry A., ed. *Becoming a Parish of Intentional Disciples*. Huntington, IN: Our Sunday Visitor, 2015.

———. *Forming Intentional Disciples: The Path to Knowing and Following Jesus*. Huntington, IN: Our Sunday Visitor, 2012.

Weigel, George. *Evangelical Catholicism: Deep Reform in the 21st-Century Church*. New York: Basic Books, 2013.

White, Michael, and Tom Corcoran. *Rebuilt: Awakening the Faithful, Reaching the Lost, and Making Church Matter*. Notre Dame, IN: Ave Maria Press, 2013.

Winesman, Albert. *Growing an Engaged Church*. New York: Gallup Press, 2007.

William E. Simon Jr. is founder and chairman of Parish Catalyst. He is the author, with Michael Novak, of *Living the Call: An Introduction to the Lay Vocation*. Simon serves as cochairman of the investment firm William E. Simon & Sons and of the William E. Simon Foundation. He is also adjunct professor in UCLA's law school and economics department.

Early in his career, Simon was an assistant US attorney in the Southern District of New York and later was the 2002 Republican gubernatorial nominee in California. For many years, he and his wife, Cindy, have helped those in need by underwriting scholarships, athletic and recreational programs, and faith-based efforts in urban areas. The Simons have four children and make their home in Los Angeles.